TESTIMONIALS

"This book will change not only the way leaders think about their role as leaders, but show them how they can execute more effectively to get the best out of their teams. If you are serious about becoming a leader that stays ahead of the curve in your industry, you must use the practical principles outlined by Anton Gunn."

—WALTER BOND
Your Next Level Coach

"This is more than a book, but a captivating reference guide. By following and applying these principles, not only will you notice a change, but so will the team that you lead. The biggest challenge to any leader is how to motivate and inspire a team to greatness, this serves as a playbook to do just that. This is a must read and perfect gift for other leaders!"

—LANCE BROWN
COO, Swype Fast

"Anton's ability to capture leadership traits in *The Presidential Principals* has already complimented my performance as a healthcare facility administrator. It's now required reading for my Interdisciplinary Leadership Team as we tackle engagement to improve clinical outcomes and employee satisfaction results."

—JERALD P. COSEY
Healthcare Facility Administrator

"I've known Anton for over twenty years and he has been a leader and an inspiration to me and many others. From leading non-profit organizations, the government, and now the private sector, his seven presidential principles have been a cornerstone for me and clients that I've consulted for many years. His writings can be used at all different levels."

–KAMAR R. JONES
Executive Management Consultant

"Anton Gunn is a force like I've never seen! His passion is evident as he offers practical and authentic direction toward effective and proven leadership practices. From drawing on the examples from past presidents to teaching the methodology to developing emerging leaders, he creates a narrative sure to equip all leaders with the necessary tools to have a lasting and maximal impact. Personally, his focused and intentional approach has positively guided and shaped my own leadership style as I transitioned from the traditional role of a physician to the role of a physician leader, and I am further encouraged to inspire others through my given service."

–CEDREK L. MCFADDEN, MD, FACS, FASCRS
Vice Chair of Clinical Affairs, Department of Surgery,
Greenville Health System

"The tools and insights Anton shares in his book have been instrumental in elevating my leadership and results. It's required reading for any leader looking to play to his or her strengths and inspire others to win. If you want to make your mark as a leader, take these principles and live them every day."

–MIA MCLEOD
South Carolina State Senator

"Unique life experiences aren't hard to find. We all have our own. What is very rare, however, is an individual with unique life experiences and an ability to share them with the masses in a way that not only teaches but inspires. Anton is that individual and this book is filled with those experiences and the lessons that have come as a result. This is a must read for any current or inspiring leader in any of our nation's service industries."

—SCOTT E. PORTER, MD, MBA, FACS, FAOA
Vice President, Organizational Equity
Professor, Department of Orthopaedic Surgery
Greenville Health System

"Anton's leadership style is more than effective—it's infective. Working with various leaders over the past twenty years, it's not hard to see why his style resonates; Anton finds the best attributes in his people and empowers them to use those skills compassionately. He's both aspirational and inspirational, something that all of our leaders could learn lessons from."

—SOL J. ROSS
Data Efficiency Strategist

"An important read for leaders at all levels. *The Presidential Principles* synthesizes the complexities of leadership development, employee engagement, and high impact sustainable results into actionable ideas which add immediate value. We are in the people business; relationships and results matter."

—JYRIC SIMS
Hospital Chief Executive Officer, FACHE

"Anton Gunn takes leadership to a new level with these principles and he provides the tools, techniques, and motivation to help every business leader. From front-line supervisor to CEO, we all can have a lasting impact. This is a must read for business leaders."

–MOSSI K. TULL
COO, Jackson and Tull

"Coaching comes easy to Anton, but leadership is truly in his DNA! I found the core principles of leadership in *The Presidential Principles: How to Inspire Action and Create Lasting Impact* both inspiring and transformational. The seven principles are like seven different lighthouses, giving you beacons to guide you today, tomorrow and years to come. Anton's book should be required reading for all who are called to serve. I now have a new book to keep on my nightstand."

–ALAN B. WILLIAMS
Member, Florida House of Representatives (2008-2016)

Christiane,
Please CADN & Make it,
Right!

THE

PRESIDENTIAL
PRINCIPLES

THE
PRESIDENTIAL
PRINCIPLES

HOW TO INSPIRE ACTION
AND CREATE LASTING IMPACT

ANTON J. GUNN

Published by Advantage, Charleston, South Carolina.
Member of Advantage Media Group.

ADVANTAGE is a registered trademark, and the Advantage colophon is a trademark of Advantage Media Group, Inc.

Printed in the United States of America.

10 9 8 7 6 5 4 3 2

ISBN: 978-1-64225-020-6
LCCN: 2018951731

Cover and layout design by Melanie Cloth.

This publication is designed to provide accurate and authoritative information in regard to the subject matter covered. It is sold with the understanding that the publisher is not engaged in rendering legal, accounting, or other professional services. If legal advice or other expert assistance is required, the services of a competent professional person should be sought.

Advantage Media Group is proud to be a part of the Tree Neutral® program. Tree Neutral offsets the number of trees consumed in the production and printing of this book by taking proactive steps such as planting trees in direct proportion to the number of trees used to print books. To learn more about Tree Neutral, please visit **www.treeneutral.com**.

Advantage Media Group is a publisher of business, self-improvement, and professional development books and online learning. We help entrepreneurs, business leaders, and professionals share their Stories, Passion, and Knowledge to help others Learn & Grow. Do you have a manuscript or book idea that you would like us to consider for publishing? Please visit **advantagefamily.com** or call **1.866.775.1696**.

This book is dedicated to the memory of my maternal grandparents, Elvin Smallwood Taylor Sr., Dorothy Paynter Taylor, and my paternal grandparents, Louis "Peter" Gunn and Evelyn Cartwright Gunn. I am your legacy.

TABLE OF CONTENTS

★ ★ ★

FOREWORD...xiii

ACKNOWLEDGEMENTS xvii

ABOUT THE AUTHOR.............................xxi

TIMELINE: In My Lifetime, Volume One xxv

INTRODUCTION: Presidential Impact 1

PART I • SERVICE

CHAPTER 1: Where I'm From 11

CHAPTER 2: Cultivate Passion, Grow
Inspiration...27

CHAPTER 3: Serve 39

PART II • EMPOWERMENT

CHAPTER 4: The Moment of Truth...........59

CHAPTER 5: Engage..................................87

CHAPTER 6: Motivate............................99

CHAPTER 7: Act....................................107

PART III • LEGACY

CHAPTER 8: What I'm Here For...............119

CHAPTER 9: Grow through Adversity.......139

CHAPTER 10: Create a Legacy of
Leadership...149

CONCLUSION: Lasting Impact.................159

Epilogue 161

References..163

Our Services 167

FOREWORD

As the mayor of Columbia, South Carolina, I consider it an honor and a privilege to lead our capital city, and I take my responsibility very seriously. I work hard not only to be successful in my role as the city's chief executive, but also to provide Columbia's residents with every opportunity to succeed.

Come to Columbia and you will find citizens from 200 countries, speaking ninety different languages. You'll find people who are creative, entrepreneurial, and committed to the same expectations of their leader as people in all other American cities. People expect their leaders to serve and empower them with the resources and opportunities to live the American dream. They expect leaders who intend to leave this world better than the way they found it and who work every day to ensure that those who come after them have more opportunities and more open doors than they did when they began their work.

These are highlights of my principles of leadership as a mayor, and they are also the same fundamental principles of great leaders around the world. That said, endorsing someone else's views on leadership is not something I do lightly. But when Anton asked me to write the foreword for this book, I said yes without any hesitation. If there is one leader who I believe can show you the importance and impact of principled leadership, it's Anton Gunn.

If you look at our respective leadership roles on paper, we are completely different. However, our goals are the same. On paper,

Anton is a leadership coach and healthcare expert working to empower leaders and their teams to make a difference in the lives of the people they serve. I am the duly elected mayor of a prospering, mid-sized Southern city, working to create the most talented, educated, and entrepreneurial city in America.

At our core, we are both keenly interested in leaving lasting impacts on the lives we have the privilege to touch. We want to deliver better services, better outcomes, and better value for the people we serve. We also believe empowering people is the integral key to better outcomes and better value. When a leader empowers those he or she serves, you unleash the power of the human spirit.

I saw this human spirit in Anton at our first meeting at the University of South Carolina when even his six-foot-five, over-275-pound frame seemed small compared to the vision, character, and leadership that immediately shined through.

As you will read, Anton understands the principles of great leadership. His smart, sincere, and thoughtful approach models the strategies he lives out each day. He understands the difference an individual can make in the lives of people, and he strives to make that difference. From our first encounter twenty-five years ago until today, Anton has done an outstanding job of demonstrating these principles in every field of human endeavor. Whether in our nation's health care industry, in government, or in the private sector, Anton's insights from America's last five presidents are inspiring and astounding. His stories and experiences have truly made an impact on my leadership journey.

Anton is one of the great thought leaders of our time. I have always been inspired by his perspectives on leadership as well as his ability to see the leadership lesson in every situation. Regardless of where you may be on your leadership journey, Anton will help you to become a better leader. His ability to educate, inspire, and empower individuals to achieve their highest potential as leaders are the qualities that make Anton one of the best in the business. This book is an investment in your potential, the culture you create, and your lasting impact. I encourage you to let the lessons in this book guide your actions as a leader. I believe if you can master these presidential principles, you will truly leave a lasting impact on the lives of those who come after you.

—STEVE BENJAMIN
Mayor, Columbia, South Carolina

ACKNOWLEDGEMENTS

I must begin by thanking my amazing wife, Tiffany, and my beautiful daughter, Ashley. From listening to me as I paced the floor of our living room speaking aloud the concept of this book, to reading early drafts, to giving me advice on the title and cover, both were instrumental in the development of this book. I am extra thankful for Tiffany as she held down our consulting business and our household so I could finish. She was just as important to this book getting done as I was. Thank you so much, babe.

Thanks to everyone on the Advantage team who helped with this project. Saara Khalil, Eland Mann, Melanie Cloth, Keven Sass, and Keith Kopcsak. Special thanks to Mark Leichliter, the man I will forever call, "Mad Skills." You turned my thoughts, concepts, and stories into a work of art. I am appreciative of our conversations and most importantly, your ability to work effortlessly with me. Special thanks to Bea Wray for your thoughtful and impactful insights on this project. I am grateful.

The conception of this book would not have been possible without many people who inspired my leadership journey. It all starts with my family, to my mother, Mona Gunn, who raised me to understand my responsibility as a leader was to be there for my younger brothers. Thank you for being a great mom and an ever-present example that we all can serve others regardless of our own personal adversities. I want to thank my brother Jamal Gunn for being the best Padawan turned Jedi Knight that I could have in my life. There was nothing more special than seeking my first publicly elected leadership position with you running the show. To my brother, Jason Gunn, thank you for being a real "Goodfella" and ensuring the legacy of the Gunn family name. To my brother, Keith Faulks, thank you for your strength of character and for reading my emails and giving me feedback. It means a lot. Most importantly, to my pops, Louge Gunn a.k.a. Foots, a.k.a. Zero, a.k.a. Sweet Lou, a.k.a. Chief Gunn. Your impact as a leader is still felt far beyond our family. We love and miss you dearly. Continue to rest in peace.

To the individuals who forged the beginning of my leadership-journey, Chuck D, Eric Jones (RIP), David Coryell, Myron Terry, Lenora Reese, John Ruoff, Marvella Caraway, Donna Dewitt, Tom Turnipseed, Pete Tepley, Gwen Hampton, Earlena Climbingbear, Rainie Jueschke, Jamaal Ferguson, Cathy Warner, Karen Gray, Karen Irick, Si Kahn, Kamau Marcharia, James Melvin Holloway, Chavice Simpkins Bush, Gilda Cobb Hunter, Joe Neal (RIP), Arlene Andrews, John Niblock, Kappy Hubbard, Cassie Hahne Barber, Anita Floyd, Emma Myers, Sue Berkowitz, Teresa Arnold, Coretta Bedsole, Bernie Mazyck, Erin Phillips Hardwick Pate, Deepak Bhargava, Jennifer Henderson, Othello Poulard, Charlene Sinclair, Kevin Borden, Erica Carter, and Errol Bolden.

I would not have been able achieve any level of success without the teams and organizations that allowed me to lead, the Zeta Epsilon Chapter of Kappa Alpha Psi, the Gamecock student athlete family at the University of South Carolina, South Carolina Fair Share, Alliance for South Carolina's Children, Grassroots Leadership, Center for Community Change, Institute for Families in Society, the Obama for America—SC team, the Department of Health and Human Services Region IV team and the Intergovernmental and External Affairs team, the Obama White House Office of Public Engagement team,

Harvard Institute of Politics team, and Fellowship Rising. The 937 Strategy Group team, Sol Ross, Sherard Duvall, Crush Rush, Kirsten Womack and Tonya Evans, and I must thank my MUSC family, especially Sarah de Barros, Stephanie Taylor, Quenton Tompkins, and Jean-Marc Villain. You each have brought out the best in me.

Extra special thanks to my best friend, James Flowers, and my boys that always hold me accountable, Jerry Inman, Keith Amos, Allen Love, Patrick Patterson, Trav Robertson, Nathaniel Smith, Malik Whitaker, and Alan Williams. Iron sharpens iron.

I also want to offer special thanks to Antoinette and Walter Bond for their valuable coaching and mentorship over the last two years. I never would have imagined our chance meeting in the Bahamas would yield so much of a harvest in my life. Your transparency, honesty, and teamwork has been the difference in my business. Thank you for teaching me how to think, execute, and win.

Finally, I want to thank Presidents George H.W. Bush, Bill Clinton, and George W. Bush. Your decisions, good and bad, large and small, have had a measurable impact on my life. Lastly, I want to thank President Barack Obama for being the archetype of how we all should carry ourselves as leaders. You are the embodiment of the principles in this book. Thank you for the example you have provided to me. Your legacy will continue to live on through my work. May God continue to bless you and your family and may God bless the United States of America.

ABOUT THE AUTHOR

Anton J. Gunn is a nationally recognized leadership consultant and healthcare reform expert. He works with individuals and organizations who want to deliver better service, better value and better outcomes for their employees and customers. He is the founder of the 937 Strategy Group, LLC, a leadership coaching and consulting practice that provides training and development services to help organizations achieve results. With more than twenty years of executive leadership experience, Anton has worked with hundreds of leaders and organizations in the public, private, and nonprofit sector. From frontline staff to the executive team, Anton has been an advisor, coach, or consultant to some of the biggest brands in America. Inspired by service and invested in empowerment, Anton's life is devoted to helping others understand the true impact of their leadership, their legacy.

Anton is former state legislator and federal policymaker playing a leadership role in many important issues. Previously, he served as one of President Barack Obama's top spokesmen on the Affordable Care Act. Anton helped the President and Health and Human Services Secretary, Kathleen Sebelius, deliver critical information during one of the most disruptive and transformational times in United States history. Anton also served as a member of the South Carolina House of Representatives from 2009-2011, becoming the first African American in South Carolina history to represent House District 79.

Anton is also a victim of Al-Qaeda's terrorism against the United States of America. His younger brother, Signalman Seaman Cherone L. Gunn was killed in the Al-Qaeda terrorist attack on the USS Cole on October 12, 2000. As a Gold Star Brother, Anton has been a powerful speaker on the impact of terrorism on his life. He shares the significance of this terrorist attack and the leadership legacy of service inspired by his brother's ultimate sacrifice in the United States Navy.

His presentations inspire leaders to think differently and act differently. Anton says he made history as a leader in sports, healthcare, and politics because he mastered the fundamentals. He learned the fundamentals growing up in a military family. He also learned them from Hip Hop music. Anton is now committed to developing more leaders by sharing the leadership principles he has learned over a lifetime. Off stage, he rolls up his sleeves with individuals and organizations to guide them through proven, easy-to-implement strategies that helps them to achieve leadership excellence.

Anton has an extensive track record in the media, including appearances in the *Los Angeles Times, Wall Street Journal, The Source Magazine, Hospitals & Health Networks Magazine, The New Yorker* and *Jet Magazine*. He also has appeared on ABC's *Good Morning America*, CBS *Evening News, MSNBC Live, TV One*, and CNN's *The Situation Room*. His leadership role in Barack Obama's campaign for president has been documented in numerous publications including *Time Magazine, The American Prospect,* and the 2010 biography, *The Bridge: The Life and Rise of Barack Obama* by David Remnick. In 2012, Anton was recognized in *The Huffington Post* as one of the Top 50 Progressive Activists Who Are Changing America.

He has lectured at more than three dozen colleges and universities including Harvard Law School, Harvard Kennedy School of Government, and the Harvard T.H. Chan School of Public Health.

He has served as a commencement speaker at Paine College, Morris Brown College and Florida A&M University. Anton is also a former adjunct faculty member at the University of South Carolina and has been an appointed board member to several state and national organizations.

He is a member of the American College of Healthcare Executives, National Speakers Association, the Aspen Institute's Aspen Global Leadership Network, and Kappa Alpha Psi Fraternity, Inc. Anton resides in South Carolina and is married to Tiffany Johnson-Gunn. They have a thirteen-year-old daughter, Ashley.

TIMELINE
IN MY LIFETIME, VOLUME ONE

MARCH 1973	Born in Portsmouth, Virginia
FEBRUARY 1978	Brother Cherone born
MAY 1980	Brothers Jason and Jamal born
JUNE 1982	Moved to Meridian, Mississippi
JUNE 1985	Moved to Chesapeake, Virginia
JANUARY 1986	Moved to Norfolk, Virginia
JUNE 1987	Moved to Virginia Beach, Virginia
JANUARY 1991	Met the 44th Vice President of the United States, Dan Quayle
JUNE 1991	Graduated from Kempsville High School (captain of football team, 1991; awarded Most Improved Player, 1991)
AUGUST 1991	Started football at the University of South Carolina
DECEMBER 1994	Graduated with BA in History

JUNE 1996	Hired at South Carolina Fair Share
JULY 1997	Hired at Alliance for South Carolina's Children
AUGUST 1998	Hired at Center for Community Change
AUGUST 1999	Started Graduate School in Social Work at the University of South Carolina
MAY 20, 2000	Married Tiffany Johnson
OCTOBER 12, 2000	Attack on the *USS Cole*; brother Cherone killed
OCTOBER 18, 2000	Met the 42nd President of the United States, Bill Clinton
MAY 2001	Graduated with MS in Social Work
JULY 2001	Hired as executive director of South Carolina Fair Share
MAY 2003	Met the 79th U.S. Attorney General, John Ashcroft, appointed by the 43rd President of the United States George W. Bush
DECEMBER 2004	Daughter Ashley born
JANUARY 31, 2004	People's Agenda for Economic Justice
NOVEMBER 6, 2006	Lost South Carolina state legislature election by 298 votes
FEBRUARY 2, 2007	Hired as South Carolina political director for Barack Obama's presidential primary campaign

NOVEMBER 4, 2008	Elected to the South Carolina House of Representatives, District 79
JANUARY 2009	Met the 44th President of the United States, Barack Obama
AUGUST 2010	Appointed by President Barack Obama to lead the regional office of Health and Human Services in Atlanta
APRIL 2012	Promoted to director of external affairs, Health and Human Services
DECEMBER 2013	Left the Obama Administration
JANUARY 2014	Founded 937 Strategy Group, LLC
AUGUST 2014	Resident fellowship, Harvard University's Institute of Politics
JANUARY 2015	Hired as executive director of Community Health Innovation and chief diversity officer at Medical University of South Carolina Health System
JUNE 2018	Met the 45th President of the United States, Donald Trump and the 48th Vice President of the United States, Mike Pence
SEPTEMBER 2018	Published *The Presidential Principles: How to Inspire Action and Create Lasting Impact*

INTRODUCTION
PRESIDENTIAL IMPACT

I have had the privilege of direct personal experience with five US presidential administrations. Not every one of those was a pleasant experience, but positive or negative, those experiences taught me important lessons about leadership. Presidents bear an unimaginable responsibility. They make decisions every day that affect millions of lives. As a result of their service, they have the capacity to have an impact, usually a lasting impact, on hundreds of millions of people and often that impact is life changing. When I look at the lessons I have learned from these personal experiences, when I study how presidents approach their role as leaders and what informs the decisions they make, I find a set of presidential leadership principles that can serve as a guide for everyone. They certainly have done so for me.

My goal in this book is to help you develop effective leadership practices that inspire action and build a lasting impact on those around you.

But what matters even more than the principles I have discovered by thinking about presidential leadership is the recognition that we all can have similar effects on the people we serve. My goal in this book is to help you develop effective leadership practices that inspire action and build a lasting impact on those around you. No matter how small or large you believe your contribution may be, you can have a presidential impact. You can have a presidential impact on your family. You can have a presidential impact on the team that you lead or on the patients you serve or on the business you are building if you commit yourself to these principles. We all can be what I call "presidential leaders," for we can all make the choice to have presidential impact *as* a leader. And those impacts can live on as a lasting legacy in the lives of those we touch.

Within this book, I turn most frequently to examples from health care, because it is the sector in which I have worked for most of my adult life, but its examples are striking because life and death stakes are so high. These principles can apply to every industry and organization in America. Nearly all face similar problems and vacuums of leadership.

Sadly, I see a disturbing trend in health care, a systemic epidemic that is like a disease ravaging hospitals and health care systems, one that is spread by leaders who do not follow the presidential leadership principles outlined in this book. We don't have to look far to see a sad irony: health care organizations should be the picture of health. However, they are extremely unhealthy. An environment where we cure disease and solve the most complex medical conditions is filled with a lot of unhealthy people. Only in recent years have hospitals passed policies to create smoke-free campuses. Enter most hospital cafeterias and you'll find the nutritional equivalent of fast food restaurants. Walk the halls and you will see sugary soft drinks in the vending machines. In stress-filled environments with twelve-hour shifts and too many patients, watch how doctors and nurses often eat. Recognize how they seldom get enough sleep. Many don't have any semblance of work-life balance.

Extend such problems into other veins and you will find an industry slow to engage their employees and face the revealing results of poor employee satisfaction. You will discover organizations diversifying their leadership teams at a snail's pace. You will see a gigantic economic sector filled with organizations that have been slow to engage patients while saying their driving force is quality patient outcomes. The reports of burnout and the numbers of doctors and nurses departing the field will astound you.

I see these problems in health care because I work within health care, but similar inabilities to engage employees or value customers exist in every industry. Such failures can all be traced back to poor leadership. A 2017 Gallup *State of the American Workplace* report drawing on all corporate sectors revealed that employees have little belief in their company's leadership.[1] They found that just 22 percent of employees strongly agree that their organization has a clear direction.

> **I see these problems in health care because I work within health care, but similar inabilities to engage employees or value customers exist in every industry. Such failures can all be traced back to poor leadership**

Eighty-five percent said that their leadership doesn't make them feel enthusiastic about the future. Seventy-seven percent reported that their organization doesn't communicate effectively.

Clearly, this country is failing in any efforts of leadership development.

---

1   "State of the American Workplace," Gallup, accessed June 25, 2018, http://news.gallup.com/reports/199961/state-american-workplace-report-2017.aspx.

There are remedies. By providing a prescription for how we can transform leadership development in the economic sector I know best—health care—we will find principles that can provide a remedy for every kind of industry and every organization that suffers parallel ailments.

The principles this book develops are not difficult in theory, but they are transformative when put into practice.

> **The events of my life have shaped the kind of leader I have become and the kind of leader for whom I advocate within these pages.**

In *The Presidential Principles: How to Inspire Action and Create Lasting Impact*, you will learn how to cultivate the passion that is within you and use it to grow inspiration within others by seeing yourself as a servant-leader: you serve those you lead rather than managing them. This book's principles are divided into three parts titled "Service," "Empowerment," and "Legacy."

- **Service**: You will learn to serve by recognizing the power that comes from engaging with those you lead, and as a result, motivating them to become accountable, proactive, reflective teams, and you will learn to further motivate them as they watch you execute your commitment to take the actions necessary to accomplish a vision for your organization.

- **Empowerment**: You will learn what is required to grow through the adversity that will inevitably accompany the bold visions you and your team develop.

- **Legacy**: You will then witness the legacy that remains in place within those you serve as they too act upon these presidential principles.

Because none of the ideas developed in this book are achievable without first actively engaging those you lead by learning and respecting their stories, along the way you will learn my own story. For the events of my life have shaped the kind of leader I have become and the kind of leader for whom I advocate within these pages.

You will also see quotes and references from hip hop music to begin each chapter. Hip hop music and culture has been instrumental to my attitude to leadership. I believe authenticity is essential to live up to your leadership potential. I would not be authentic if I did not share how hip hop has influenced my leadership journey. Additionally, in this book, I mention many of the books that have helped in my development as leader, and I have provided a reference section listing important books for leadership development. I hope they hold as much value for you as they have for me.

Before you are done with this book, it is my hope that you will begin to see how you can have a presidential impact within your organization and help transform the lives and careers of those you serve with

> **I would not be authentic if I did not share how hip hop has influenced my leadership journey.**

your leadership. In the process, you will find yourself empowered as well and you will discover new satisfaction and internal reward, renewing the passion that motivated you to seek leadership in the first place.

SEVEN PRESIDENTIAL PRINCIPLES

★ ★ ★

1 INSPIRE OTHERS THROUGH YOUR ACTION

Your leadership must lead. Be a verb and not a noun. Your actions as a leader will always be more important than your words.

2 ANSWER THE CALL TO SERVICE

You must choose to serve those you hope to lead. Serve them first, lead them second.

3 DECIDE TO ENGAGE

You should listen, think, and then act. Be intentional in the practice of listening, learning, and caring about those you lead.

4 BE A GREAT MOTIVATOR

You must use words, emotions, tools, and tactics to be a catalyst. Your daily deeds must focus on moving people to action.

5 PREACH WHAT YOU KNOW

Always tell your story and share why you have chosen to lead. You must communicate with transparency, authenticity, and clarity.

6 ACCEPT ACCOUNTABILITY AND SHARE RESPONSIBILITY

When things go wrong you must own the accountability for the failure. When things go well, you must share the responsibility of the success.

7 WORK TODAY FOR TOMORROW'S IMPACT

Successful leaders make decisions for today. Significant leaders make decisions for tomorrow. You must choose to be significant to have a lasting impact.

PART I

★ ★ ★

SERVICE

Everybody can be great because everybody can serve.

—Dr. Martin Luther King, Jr.

CHAPTER 1
WHERE I'M FROM

I'm up the block, round the corner, and down the street …

—Jay Z, "Where I'm From"

E veryone has a story. If you are able to tell your life story, then you can speak to what is important to you. If you can under- stand where you come from and what makes you who you are, then you can be effective at helping others know how to motivate you. To understand my vision of leadership, you need to know where I come from. This is my story. And this is where my choice to become an impactful leader begins.

When I was thirteen, music was everything to me. This was the golden age of hip hop and every new single offered something innovative: the age of Run–DMC, Public Enemy, the Beastie Boys … I thought I was going to be the next LL Cool J. I loved the music and I lived hip hop culture: shell toe Adidas, Pumas, Levi jeans, bomber jackets, Gucci sweatshirts,

> **To understand my vision of leadership, you need to know where I come from.**

Coca Cola shirts … If my grandma gave me twenty dollars for getting a grade of A in English, I would use that to buy the same Adidas that Run-DMC wore or the jacket The Fat Boys owned. I immersed myself in hip hop culture. It defined an important part of who I was and who I remain. Every Tuesday, I walked from my house to my sanctuary—DJ's Records and Tapes—because Tuesdays were when new music came out. And on a summer Tuesday when Public Enemy's "It Takes a Nation of Millions to Hold Us Back" was released, my world changed forever.

I wasn't a bad kid, but I'd begun to hang around a lot of bad kids. Staying out too late or not coming home when it got dark, those are the things that I would get in trouble for. But earlier on that Tuesday, I ended up in the backseat of a stolen midnight blue IROC Z-28.

My family had moved back to Norfolk, Virginia—my childhood home and the place my parents had met—earlier that year after a few years in Mississippi and six months in Chesapeake. The school I transferred to with the move was the feeder middle school for the elementary school I attended before we left. So, I was reunited with some of my old friends. When I came back,

I ended up in the backseat of a stolen midnight blue IROC Z-28.

it was as if kids I knew from kindergarten were seeing me as a thirteen-year-old for the first time, but it meant I had friends, something I'd struggled with in the previous months. The neighborhood where I had lived as a child had gotten worse during the Reagan era. Some of the kids I had known in kindergarten were now smoking weed, stealing cars, robbing 7-Elevens, and going to jail and to juvenile hall. I started to fall in with some of them. Mostly, I just succumbed to peer pressure, going along with the crowd. For me, falling into trouble was crime of opportunity because my mom was teaching school and my dad was out to sea as a sailor in the navy. And, of course, at thirteen, I was girl crazy, and the nice girls liked the bad boys. So, the badder I could be, the cooler I was.

Which is how I ended up in the backseat of a stolen car in a high-speed chase. My joyriding friends, who were older—sixteen and seventeen to my fourteen—had spent time in juvenile hall, but I'd never been in real trouble and I was scared to death. Every black boy I know is scared of police officers, and I wasn't thinking about regret or thinking about anything other than I was afraid. Yet even in that moment, I was more frightened of my dad finding out than what the police would do to me. My dad could be a hard man—if you looked up "cuss like a sailor" in the dictionary, my dad's picture would be beside it. He literally used to say stuff like, "If I catch you doing anything wrong, I will kill you." It wasn't that he was joking. I believed him to be serious because he would follow it up and say, "And it don't matter to me because I can make another child that looks just like you."

When we got caught in that stolen car, I wanted the police to put me in jail for twenty-five years. I hoped my parents would feel sorry for me rather than have my dad find out.

There I was. In a stolen car. Bad choices catching up with me. My friends decided to run. We were next to the cemetery near my neighborhood and thought we could get away. I was going through a growth spurt and never made it out of the seatbelt. We all were arrested. They put us in three separate police cars, took us to the police station, and put us in separate holding rooms.

I was sitting there, scared to death, when the cop walked in, African American, balding, mid-to-late forties, wearing a tie—clearly, he was a detective—and I knew I was done. But God stepped into that situation, because the cop took the cuffs off, grabbed me by my arm, and took me out into an open area where he sat me down in a chair. He pulled another chair up in front of me and said, "You're lucky we got the story from your friends, and I'm going to tell you, you need to stop hanging around these bad kids, because if you keep hanging around them, you're going to end up in jail. Do you want to go to jail?"

I said, "No, sir."

"Do you want to spend your life in prison?"

"No, sir."

"Then why are you hanging around with guys who steal cars? You're lucky you didn't know it was stolen. We got the story. They're in trouble. But we're going to give you a second chance. We're going to let you go."

They let me walk out of the police station. Didn't call my parents. I can't even remember if I gave them my full name.

Since it was Tuesday, on my way home I walked into DJ's Records and Tapes, and it was as if everything that had happened before that point didn't matter anymore, because I was safely and securely in my sanctuary. I walked to the back of the store where they kept the hip hop, because despite being a home to dee jays, hip hop wasn't yet very commercial. I went right to the new releases. I was flipping through the new vinyl and I saw this album that forever changed my life. It was shiny with the plastic over it, and it showed two black men in a jail cell. At the time, hip hop artists didn't look like that. They wore gold chains and fly sweat suits and

> "We're going to give you a second chance. We're going to let you go."

sat on the front of Mercedes Benzes, or they were Run DMC in their Cadillac. They were styling. But these two guys weren't trying to style. They had on baseball caps and Starter jackets and Raiders hats, clocks around their neck—the expected parts of hip hop culture—but they were behind bars. The top of the album said, "Public Enemy," and along the right side, it said, "It Takes a Nation of Millions to Hold Us Back." Looking at that cover, staring at those prison bars when I thought I might be going to prison, I was filled with questions. What made them a public enemy? Who was trying to hold them back? What were they saying? I had to have that music because I needed answers to those questions.

Or at least that's how I remember it now, the terror of being taken to the police station and the escape of returning to the sanctuary of the record store all wrapped up together. Those events became one for me—like two sides of the same coin—as I look back on them more than thirty years later. What I know for sure is that the questions that filled my mind still linger and the effects of listening to that music have helped guide my life.

What I remember with certainty is buying the cassette and putting on my headphones. The tape started, and there was this loud crash and clash of music and different sounds and then Chuck D screaming, "… back is the incredible rhyme animal, the untenable D, Public enemy number one." I know those lyrics word for word to this day. I listened closely to the stories of how black people in American continued to be systematically held back by prejudicial treatment and called for black self-empowerment. The songs told me that I could be a part of the problem or be a part of the solution and that the only way I could protect myself was to develop my mind. Public Enemy told me that an educated black man is the most dangerous thing in the world. Those words spoke to my existence.

I didn't stop at the lyrics. I opened the cassette case and read the credits where I encountered names I'd never heard before. The liner notes talked about Farrakhan, Ida B. Wells, Jesse Jackson. I wondered: "Who are these people, and what is this about?" I didn't have any context for such references. I listened to the words, "Farrakhan is a prophet that I think that you should listen to because what he can say to you is what you ought to do,"[2] and I didn't even know who Farrakhan was. For all I knew he taught Chuck D how to rap.

Public Enemy told me that an educated black man is the most dangerous thing in the world. Those words spoke to my existence.

I caught the city bus to the public library, where I started researching every person who was listed in the credits of Public Enemy's album. I thought, *These must be some powerful people if Chuck D is giving them credits inside of his liner notes.* I started reading everything I could find. I picked up *A Message to a Black Man in America* by Elijah Muhammad and started to read. I found myself inside a litany of Black Nationalist rhetoric teaching me that I needed to get my act together. I had intelligence. I had capabilities. I read texts that told me I had the ability to do anything I wanted to do, that I didn't have to fall victim to the wicked ways of the world or be subjugated to government oppression or racial politics. Those books led me to other books, including the novel that remains my all-time favorite *The Spook Who Sat by the Door* by Sam Greenlee, the story of first black man in the CIA, who, after being trained in guerrilla warfare, weaponry, communications, and subversion, resigns and

---

2   "Bring the Noise," MP3 audio, track 2 on Public Enemy, *It Takes a Nation of Millions to Hold Us Back*, Def Jam Recordings, 1998.

fights on the behalf of African Americans. That book became an internal battle cry for me to become physically, mentally, emotionally prepared to meet the future and fight for social justice.

In the months and years after the release of *It Takes a Nation of Millions to Hold Us Back* and the second chance given to me by that police detective, I was ingesting all of this music and culture and black nationalist rhetoric, and I began paying attention to politics. I was listening to artists and really hearing the lyrics, not taking them literally word for word but distilling the messages. Chuck D replied in an interview with Def Jam Recordings, when asked if his goal was to go platinum, that he didn't care about a platinum album; he wanted to create 5,000 new black leaders working in the community.[3] And when I heard that, I made the decision that I was going to be involved. That is when I first saw a life of service. So hip hop is my first political memory. Hip hop is what got me involved and engaged and where I formed my social conscience and my political awareness.

> **That is when I first saw a life of service. So hip hop is my first political memory. Hip hop is what got me involved and engaged and where I formed my social conscience and my political awareness.**

3   Greg Kot, "Chuck D.'s Public Enemy Fights Power of Racism," *Sun Sentinel*, last modified July 29, 1990, http://articles.sun-sentinel.com/1990-07-29/features/9002060375_1_chuck-d-s-black-planet-new-black-leaders.

Not that I should have needed to get in trouble to be jarred to awareness. I had never been short of good role models in my life. My mother was a career teacher who later rose to become a principal. My father was a US Navy petty officer. My aunt Nancy was a nurse. She served people every day of her life, and after working exhausting twelve-hour shifts caring for others, she never hesitated to care for us when my mom needed her help because my dad was away at sea. She did everything from changing a diaper to babysitting me and my three brothers to taking us to the movies. My grandfather was a man of honor, a World War II veteran and committed to mattering to people. A man of goodwill, he wasn't just successful; he was significant, whether in people's memories from the years he excelled in negro league baseball or when he volunteered his expertise as an electrician to the people of his neighborhood.

My mom, the second oldest daughter in a family of ten children, grew up poor. When her older brother and sister each left home at eighteen, she was responsible for helping her mother with her siblings, everything from dressing them to doing their hair to getting them ready for school. That is her personality: the responsible one who takes charge. Her dad worked multiple jobs to make ends meet and to make sure that his children could go to good schools. Because of his commitment, my mother went to Catholic school where she graduated in a class that included only a handful of students of color, but that parochial education gave her a lot of things, including exposure to people outside her community. She was a straight-A student, a hard worker, the sort who was always disciplined and focused. From high school she went to a historically black college, Norfolk State University, where she majored in education.

She started teaching in 1974, spending most of her time as an elementary teacher. Later in her career, teaching at a school with a great principal who saw her leadership potential and wanted to invest in her development, she felt encouraged to go back and get her master's degree in education from Old Dominion University. From there, she took on more and more leadership roles in the schools where she served, becoming a Title I specialist in schools in public housing neighborhoods where parental involvement was hardly existent and where she saw how she could have an impact on students' lives by creating programming that gave them educational opportunities. She continued to grow in her role as a leader and became an assistant principal and eventually, a principal.

She spent a career leading schools and inspiring teachers. One of my middle school classmates, Nicole Moore, became a teacher underneath my mom at Fair Lawn Elementary. Nicole is quick to say that she's a principal today because of the leadership development my mom gave her as a young teacher and the nurturing and mentorship and investment my mom offered her. My mom was this way in every aspect of her life. She was service oriented and helpful, but at the same time, sociable and magnetic.

Her passion and leadership extended far beyond the school walls. In the years before we returned to Norfolk, my dad was transferred to the naval air station in Meridian, Mississippi. As soon as my mom gained her certification to teach in Mississippi, she was back inside a fifth-grade classroom. Then, in 1985, she joined teachers from four districts who defied a temporary court order and participated in the first teacher strike in Mississippi history. At the time, Mississippi teachers were paid 20 percent less than their peers, as calculated from an average rating in poor-paying regions of eleven states.[4] I remember seeing a TV news broadcast showing my mom holding a protest sign, and, even at ten years old, I saw that she stood up for herself and she was outspoken and true to her beliefs.

My image of my mom is that, for thirty years, all she did was serve other people's families by developing and educating their kids. My mom empowered those around her including other teachers like Nicole, and gave them the skills and the tools to accomplish more.

Now, in contrast, if you had met my dad about the time my mom did, he might have looked more like the version of me arrested for joyriding than like the man who ended up becoming an inspiration to countless navy personnel. As a young man, my dad was infamous before he was famous, a knucklehead of epic proportions.

He grew up in a working-class neighborhood called Cavalier Manor. There's a book written by Nathan McCall titled *Makes Me Wanna Holler* and the first chapter is about my dad's neighborhood. Before McCall was a journalist, he was a convicted felon. In the book, he talks about the older guys in the neighborhood who showed him how to be a hoodlum. He references my dad and his friends. When I attended a book signing, I told McCall that I was Louge Gunn's son. He looked at me in amazement because he assumed my dad was either dead or in jail and there was no way that he'd have a son on a college campus at a book signing.

That was my dad as a young man. He failed to graduate high school, completing his GED two years later. Eventually, he got himself arrested, and my grandfather went to the police station, picked him up, and said, "I'm not coming down to jail to bail you out anymore. You've got two choices. You can stay in this jail cell or you can join the military." So, my dad joined the US Navy. That decision was the

---

4   "Teachers Strike in Mississippi," *The New York Times*, February 26, 1985, https://www.nytimes.com/1985/02/26/us/teachers-strike-in-mississippi.html.

best thing that ever happened to him because it made a man out of him. He met my mom once he joined the navy, and then, over a twenty-two-year career, he retired as a chief petty officer.

If you know anything about the navy, you understand that no naval ship can function without strong chief petty officers. They are the enlisted leaders of a ship. As a chief petty officer, my dad earned his stripes by serving the sailors on the ship, gaining their respect, investing in them, being perceptive about their needs. No one rises to any level of leadership in the US Navy without hard work and dedication to the other men and women who serve alongside them. My father passed away in February 2016 from lung cancer; 1,500 people attended his funeral. There were guys who served with him who spoke at my dad's wake and said things such as, "If it wasn't for Chief Gunn in my life, I would never have made it twenty years in the navy," and "I wouldn't have finished my degree without his advice; I wouldn't have gone to college and used my GI Bill." My dad would give his last for anyone. He would help people buy a car. He would let people stay with us when they were down on their luck. He let people borrow money. His own finances could be in shambles, but he'd use his own money to help other people.

When my father retired from the navy, times became hard for him. At forty-two, he was diagnosed with diabetes and sarcoidosis. He couldn't find a job. He had spent twenty-two years in the navy and yet he struggled to receive his veteran's benefits. At one point early in his retirement, he found work as a security guard at a shipyard and while he was on that job, a ship on which he had been an enlisted officer was in dry dock. There he was, a security guard—no real badge, no gun, just a uniform jacket, sitting outside the shipyard gate for an hourly wage. He later went from there to working in a 7-Eleven. But instead of giving up, my dad became passionate about veterans' issues. He could not stand to see veterans struggle the way he struggled. He went back to school and earned both a bachelor's and a master's degree in social work. He went to work for the state division of the US Department of Veteran's Affairs as a counselor, and eventually, worked his way up to the federal Department of Veterans Affairs. He was the president of a Disabled American Veterans chapter in Virginia Beach. When Barack Obama was running for president in 2008, Joe Biden came to Virginia and held a town hall meeting on veterans' issues, and my dad was asked to sit on the panel. He had cache. He had a way about himself.

Just as my mom used her innate pursuit of responsibility, seized opportunities, and emerged a leader, my dad used his strength of personality and drive to help people to do the same. Together they endured something that would have broken most people. My brother, Cherone, was killed in the terrorist attack on the *USS Cole* in October 2000, while the ship was refueling in Yemen.

> **Just as my mom used her innate pursuit of responsibility, seized opportunities, and emerged a leader, my dad used his strength of personality and drive to help people to do the same.**

Everybody talks about the difficulty of a parent losing a child and how devastating that is; my family lived it firsthand. I lived it watching my mom struggle to continue to educate other people's children and to nurture other teachers while she was in great pain and grieving. She showed me what resilience is all about and how you face adversity. After Cherone was killed, my mom became involved in the American Gold Star Mothers Incorporated, a ninety-year-old organization founded by mothers who have lost children in military service. The purpose of the Gold Star Mothers is to support veterans' organizations and to create support mechanisms for gold star families, but their informal mission is to build a bond with moms who share an unthinkable thing in common. My mom first became involved at the local level, and then she became the local chapter president. Eventually, at the national level, she was the second African American ever to serve on the board of directors in the organization's history. In 2017 she was elected to the position of second vice president and will become the organization's president after a two-year term. Her presidency will start in 2019 and end in 2020, which will be the twenty-year anniversary of the *USS Cole* attack and the loss of my brother. My mom has already planned to have the Gold Star Mother Convention in Virginia Beach, Virginia, our hometown.

As you can see, I have known leaders all my life. I've had numerous role models, from family members to hip hop stars to coaches and teachers to a detective who intervened when he saw the potential in someone.

Despite my exposure to meaningful leaders, I needed intervention when I was a teen. When my family first returned to Virginia from Mississippi, we rented a house for six months in Chesapeake. This was about as low a point in my life as I had ever experienced until then. I had just entered puberty. Girls were getting cute. I was awkward. I didn't have the fancy clothes that everybody else was wearing. I didn't have the haircuts or the jewelry or the medallions. My parents shopped at the navy commissary and the navy exchange, so I wore straight-legged jeans with super starch creases, courtesy of my dad. I was shy. I lacked confidence. I was a fish out of water in that suburb, with no real friends and very few people who looked like me.

We lived on the same corner as the school bus stop. When school started that fall of 1985, I was so afraid of the other kids that I would stay in the house and look out the window until I saw the bus pull up, and then I would get on the bus and sit in the front seat so I didn't have to see anybody behind me. When it rained, all of the kids gathered on our porch and waited for the bus. I would be inside the house, television off, music off, leaning against the window, listening to their conversations, too scared to join in.

> **I have known leaders all my life. I've had numerous role models, from family members to hip hop stars to coaches and teachers to a detective who intervened when he saw the potential in someone.**

The only thing I excelled at in those six months was football. Playing football at Deep Creek Junior High is how I made friends. Football felt like the only thing I had.

But then we moved back to Norfolk. Back to the old neighborhood and all my old friends. No more football and I was now running with the wrong crowd and getting bad grades. I had earned As and Bs in Chesapeake and was placed in classes for gifted students. In Norfolk I was getting Ds and Fs. You've seen where that got me.

I don't know if my parents had seen what was happening to me in Norfolk, but we moved to Virginia Beach. My transition from eighth grade in Norfolk to ninth grade in Virginia Beach was like going from the movie *Lean on Me* to the TV show *Saved by the Bell*. I remember that in Norfolk, when I was at Lake Taylor Middle School, there were three white kids. One of the administrators was white, but I don't remember a single white teacher's name. However, when I went to Kempsville in Virginia Beach, I moved into a much more diverse school, though one mostly of white kids. So, it was culture shock for me. Radical, pro-black hip hop music was the only thing that grounded me to my culture and community. It felt like the only thing I had left that was part of me.

That summer, I grew like a giant. I went from five feet ten inches and 185 pounds to six feet three inches and 220 pounds. My mom said, "You need to be playing football." She took me to Kempsville Junior High School where they were already practicing. I walked onto the practice field and the coach, Tim Spruill, looked at me and said, "You're on the team. Can you practice today?" I had on a polo shirt and a red Kangol hat like the one LL Cool J used to wear. They wore full pads and equipment, and I wore sneakers. My mom answered the coach for me, "Yeah, you ain't got nothing to do." I practiced with them in my sneakers and polo shirt. The only thing I did was take off my Kangol.

Our team sucked. We lost every game. I played fullback. I played tight end. I was a kick returner. I was the punter one week. I was the middle linebacker one week. Football gave me identity in a strange school. But that whole first semester I was feeling sorry for myself. I was mad at my parents for moving. I didn't like any of the kids I was in school with, mostly white kids, a few Filipinos, and one or two black kids who grew up in the suburbs with parents who had great jobs and nice cars while I was a working-class kid.

But I began to think back on that summer and the trouble I had gotten into and the reading I was doing and the music I loved. Public Enemy gave me a framework that I was going to use for the rest of my life. About the same time, the movie *Heartbreak Ridge* came out. Clint Eastwood played Gunnery Highway, an old Korean veteran sergeant who didn't take crap, and they gave him the worst unit ever: a bunch of misfits. Some had been in jail. Others had gone AWOL. What Gunnery Highway taught them is three words I still use in almost every talk or speech I give: improvise, adapt, and overcome. A child of a tough military father, those words spoke to me.

With Gunnery Highway telling me to improvise, adapt, and overcome, and Chuck D saying I needed to "become a rebel without a pause," I learned how to operate in any kind of environment. I had read *The Spook Who Sat by the Door* and made the decision that I needed to become friendly with everyone. I needed to learn what else suburban kids could teach me about how to be successful and use that to better my community. I went from being the angry kid on the football team to finishing my ninth-grade year with the vote of "friendliest student."

> **What Gunnery Highway taught them is three words I still use in almost every talk or speech I give: improvise, adapt, and overcome.**

As I entered high school, I had learned to listen to leaders and to hear the lessons they offered. I wasn't ready to be a leader yet, but I had formed the framework. I had role models telling me I needed to better myself and serve my community and I had grown up in an environment that taught me how to improvise, adapt, and overcome, essential qualities I would develop on my leadership journey. I had learned how to tell my story.

CHAPTER 2
CULTIVATE PASSION, GROW INSPIRATION

Teachers teach and do the world good. Kings just
rule and most are never understood.

—Boogie Down Productions, "My Philosophy"

My first full-time job after college was working for a nonprofit organization called South Carolina Fair Share. I had no reason to get the job. I had no meaningful work experience. I had been a history major and had never worked in public policy or health care. When I interviewed for the job, I didn't even own a sports jacket. But I got the job because a complete stranger took a chance on me. That stranger became a lifelong mentor. Her name is Lenora Bush Reese. Looking back, twenty years later, perhaps Lenora saw something in me. Perhaps she saw passion.

> **I got the job because a complete stranger took a chance on me. That stranger became a lifelong mentor.**

I don't know, but she took the time to learn my story, and then, she invested in me.

Lenora is so important to my development as a leader that she will figure prominently in this book. Many of the presidential principles I can pass along are embodied in Lenora and from the moment I started working for her, I was inspired by her. She was the executive director of South Carolina Fair Share, a statewide, multi-issue advocacy and community-organizing nonprofit that investigated public policy, identified solutions, and worked for social change for mostly low-income people of color residing in rural communities. I saw Lenora's passion for social justice and immediately, I wanted to demonstrate my willingness to show that her faith in me was not misplaced.

Even then, out of college for eighteen months, depressed because I couldn't find a job, back living with my parents, a hip hop militant who had dabbled in college activism mostly around fair treatment for college athletes, I saw Lenora's ability to inspire. She inspired me every day as I watched how she worked with people and how she shared herself and her expertise. As all great inspirational leaders know, she also knew how to transfer her passion and her energy to the people around her. She knew how to motivate people into taking action.

I really do believe that everyone has a purpose. In order for you to figure out your purpose, there are two things that you've got to discover: what you are passionate about and what you are good at.

When I say, "passion," I'm asking about that thing that makes you get out of bed in the morning. What is that thing that inspires you, motivates you, makes you angry, makes you smile, and gives meaning to your life? It might be just about anything so long as it is genuine.

Once you identify your passions, you have to learn what you are good at. What is the skill set you possess that you can use to master your passions? Being passionate alone is not good enough; you've got become an expert about your passion. You have to learn more about your subject matter than anyone else and cultivate that passion. We all have passions, but becoming an expert at what you love will help to define your purpose. Then, you have to show the will to move beyond being good at it. How do you become great at

I really do believe that everyone has a purpose. In order for you to figure out your purpose, there are two things that you've got to discover: what you are passionate about and what you are good at.

it? Because you will quickly learn that when you are truly passionate about something in your life, you become willing to work harder, learn more, push yourself harder than anybody else, and became an expert. The people who master their passions demand the biggest presence, and they gain the biggest opportunity to show their greatness.

As you cultivate your passion and master the subject areas it takes you to, you will learn how to share it. That light that shines inside you is your passion, and you've got to project that light to other people because that's what they gravitate to. The light of your passion pushes the darkness away. You bring light to dark spaces when you know what you are passionate about and you share your passion.

Passion is your internal flame. It burns inside you. The best leaders not only know how to light their own fires; they know how to stoke the fire in others and they stoke that fire with inspiration. Great leaders can provide an unlimited supply of oxygen to the people who follow them. When a team becomes exhausted, when they are defeated by temporary setbacks, when they get told no by others, their leader is the one who gives them the inspiration to take the next step. Your inspiration needs to be tangible to everyone who follows you. They may not share your passion, but they should always love your inspiration. They can draw inspiration from you, based upon how you share what you are passionate about. When people see how passionate I am about health care or about hip hop, their own passion increases, whatever it may be.

As a leader, it's your responsibility to share, teach, learn, and help those around you to figure out what they are passionate about and what they are good at so that they ultimately discover their purpose. Part of your job is to give people something to take action on. That's inspiration.

> **Passion is your internal flame. It burns inside you. The best leaders not only know how to light their own fires; they know how to stoke the fire in others and they stoke that fire with inspiration.**

I have four primary passions in my life. I'm passionate about leadership. I'm passionate about health care. I'm passionate about young people and professional development in young people, and I'm passionate about hip hop. Those four things make me get up in the morning. I discovered my love for hip hop when I was ten, became passionate about leadership at sixteen when I saw the need for leadership on my football team. I found a passion for health care at the age of twenty-three, and for the professional development of young people at thirty. It takes time to find your passion. It might take you decades. Colonel Harland Sanders didn't start Kentucky Fried Chicken until he was sixty-five, and he impacted an entire industry by his actions.[5] There's no shelf life for being a great leader. There's no shelf life for being the best you. Always remember you have until the day you take your last breath to get better.

I didn't recognize my passion for health care until I was out in the community, hearing people's stories, working to help improve their lives. The truth was that prior to that, I was oblivious to the realities facing people trying to gain health insurance coverage and get access to health care. Growing up, I didn't have to give health care a lot of thought because my family always had access to good health care through the navy and through the school district. I was a healthy kid. So, mostly, beyond routine yearly physicals for sports, I had no reason to give access to health care a thought. Once I started college, I was a Division I football player at a major Southeastern Conference (SEC) university, so I had full access to health care, and the University of South Carolina covered the cost. If I got a cold while I was in college, I just went to the training room, found the team physician, and fifteen minutes later, he gave me a prescription for a Z-pack, which I simply handed to another member of the staff to fill. During my red-shirt junior

As a leader, it's your responsibility to share, teach, learn, and help those around you to figure out what they are passionate about and what they are good at so that they ultimately discover their purpose.

5   "Colonel Harland Sanders," Biography, accessed June 25, 2018, https://www.biography.com/people/colonel-harland-sanders-12353545.

year, I hurt my back playing football, and they ordered two MRIs to determine the damage. Whether it was an MRI or a broken toe or a sprained wrist or any of the injuries expected for college football players, I never once lacked care and I never once saw a medical bill. So, I was beyond naïve about what most people faced when trying to receive health care.

After I graduated college, I spent a year working in temporary jobs and going to interviews as I tried to get a full-time job. I had no regular doctor. I had no insurance. I was so naïve, so used to having access that in July of that year, the time I always associated with getting a routine physical, I tried to get an appointment for a check-up. After being told they didn't have any appointment availability for two weeks, I was asked if I had insurance and when I told them I did not, I was told, "Well, you can't come to us for a primary care visit without being insured." I told the woman serving me that I was healthy and just wanted to make sure that I stayed healthy. She replied that they didn't do physicals because the insurance companies would not reimburse for physicals. Now, if something was wrong with me, they'd be happy to do a physical. The woman said, "We can't see you because, one, you don't have insurance and, two, because there's nothing wrong with you." I thought this was the most ridiculous thing. Was I ever in for a surprise. When I went to work for Fair Share, I was reminded daily of my naivety about the nature of health care.

So, my passion for health care was one I had to discover. As I faced the realities of gaining access to health care myself, and as I worked in poor communities where many of the people I met had never had routine medical care, I found a passion I didn't know existed within me.

A lot of us don't know what we're passionate about right away, but we all have something we love doing. Passion may start with whatever we enjoy doing more than anything else. It could be anything and following one passion may lead us to another. When Lenora hired me, she sent me to work as a community organizer, feeding my innate desire to connect with people and to hear their stories. This work built on my abilities to adapt to new situations and environments, and I dug in and discovered in depth the issues facing the people we were trying to help. I listened to their stories and learned about their lives, and I placed what I had learned within the context of the policy issues we were advocating.

All this time, my passion for hip hop never diminished, and I would hear the lyrics of songs as I entered communities where I worked. I would enter public housing communities and see sixteen-year-olds not finishing high school because, at fourteen years of age, they had had a baby, curtailing their school education and limiting

> **All this time, my passion for hip hop never diminished, and I would hear the lyrics of songs as I entered communities where I worked.**

their professional opportunities. A song such as "Teenage Love" by Slick Rick or "Brenda's Got a Baby" by Tupac Shakur would play in my head, providing me with another context and motivating me to try to develop programs that could help them. When I worked on the 1996 Telecommunications Act about phone service in rural communities, I learned emergency services couldn't always find callers because they didn't have a street address, and I could hear Public Enemy's "911 is a Joke" in my head. There was always a hip hop undertone, a theme song related to my organizing days, one passion fueling another passion and inspiring me to act on the behalf of social justice.

As I cultivated my passion, I did everything in my power to learn how to be an effective community organizer and an expert on policy issues affecting the people I served. I learned that I was really good at telling a story and connecting complex subjects to everyday life. I could take a complex piece of public policy, such as the Landlord-Tenant Act, and break it down in a way that someone with a sixth-grade education could understand. I became adept at speaking to diverse audiences on various issues and helping them understand how they could use such information to better their own lives. Later in life, when I worked with the White House on health care reform, I was called on to do presentations on the Affordable Care Act (ACA) because I could break it down in a way that anybody can understand. Lenora had inspired me with her passion and helped me discover my own.

Your passions will be different from mine, but they are what will drive you to excellence and to your purpose in life. You have to give your passions time and attention and grow to be an expert in them. To do so, you not only have to cultivate knowledge; you need to seek out mentors. You can only learn by turning to those who can teach from their experience. Those mentors will help you succeed. You will benefit from learning the lessons available to you from the leaders around you. And then you have to use your expertise and leadership to benefit others and excel in your role. You have people in your life who have inspired you. Cultivate your passions and you will inspire others as well.

PRESIDENTIAL PRINCIPLE NUMBER ONE
Inspire Others through Your Action

The lessons that President Obama taught me by his example on how to be an inspirational leader started long before I met him. In 2006 I had just lost an election for the South Carolina State legislature by 298 votes. I was bitter about the loss even though others around me were celebrating that I had come so close to winning in a Republican-dominated district that had never elected an African American. I felt I was a good candidate who had the right message and was reaching people. Shortly after the election, I went to DC for a meeting at the Center for Community Change, and in the meeting, Greg Galluzzo, a Jesuit Priest from Chicago, said, "Barack Obama might run for president." I'd never heard of him. I had never seen him speak. I didn't see his Democratic Convention speech in 2004. I said, "Nobody in the United States of America is going to vote for a black man named Barack Hussein Obama."

After the meeting, I was in Reagan National Airport, where I walked into the bookstore closest to my gate. Immediately, I saw on display a copy of *The Audacity of Hope* by Barack Obama. I thought, *Oh, this is the guy who's going to run for president. Let me see what he's about.* And the next thing I know is that I'm so engrossed in the book that I missed my flight home. I bought the book and the audio version, and on the rebooked flight home, I listened to his voice as I read his words. What took me aback was that he was saying the same things I was trying to say when I was running for the legislature. However, he was much more compelling and much more authentic in his stories about the experiences of people and the encounters he had had with the average American. I felt an immediate kinship. He was a community organizer. He not only learned how to listen to people's stories but also connect those stories to what other people were going through. I lost the election because I hadn't read the book.

He had the power to inspire me even from his book. I made the decision that I was going to get involved in his campaign. It was work I wanted to do even as I was again running for the state legislative seat in 2008.

> **I felt an immediate kinship. He was a community organizer. He not only learned how to listen to people's stories but also connect those stories to what other people were going through. I lost the election because I hadn't read the book.**

I could share a thousand stories about my experiences with Barack Obama and his ability to be an inspirational leader, but after serving on his campaign for thirteen months, there is one moment that stands out above all others in my mind: November 3, 2008, the day before the election. I hadn't seen him in person since that January, when he won the South Carolina democratic primary by a margin of 28.9 percent.[6] He had, of course, gone on to win the national primary and now faced election day in a campaign against John McCain. While I was in the midst of the final run-up to my own legislative election, I knew Barack was going to lead a rally in Charlotte and I wanted to be there to support him, so I called Reggie Love, and I said, "I'm coming to Charlotte because I just want to shake Barack's hand before he faces election day." Later that day the news broke that his grandmother, Madelyn Dunham, "Toot," had

---

6   "South Carolina Primary Results," *The New York Times*, accessed June 25, 2018, https://www.nytimes.com/elections/2008/primaries/results/states/SC.html.

died at the age of eighty-six from cancer. She had raised Obama from the time he was ten years old and was the matriarch of the family, someone Obama later labeled as a woman of extraordinary accomplishment, strength, and humility. Anyone could have understood that since he had only just learned of her passing, he would not have wanted to be bothered with people or be energetic.

I went to Charlotte. It was an outdoor rally, and it was pouring rain. I arrived early. When Barack reached the backstage tent, he was surprised to see me. He greeted me with our typical embrace: shook my hand, gave me the brother handshake, and a one-armed hug. He looked at me and said, "How are you doing?"

I replied, "Don't worry about how I'm doing. How are you doing?"

"I'm hurting," he said, "but I know that I'm supposed to be here and that I've got to win this election. So I'm going to go out here and give this speech. I'll see you when I come back."

He gave an emotional, memorable speech. I sat in the back, listening closely but also absorbing all of the things that he had to put up with for the entire campaign. Not just that moment of losing his grandmother, but all the assaults from the very beginning, which included people calling him a Muslim and claiming he snorted cocaine, the Clintons' attempt to demean him in the primary, suggesting he couldn't win, and the Republican Party's attempt to demonize him and make him seem to be something he's not. He had never seemed fazed.

I knew he was hurting. I could see the exhaustion in his face. I noticed the slight droop of his tired eyes. But what I saw more than anything else was a man destined to persevere through whatever adversity came at him. Watching him was probably the seminal essence of why I know I can achieve anything because I cannot imagine running for president of the United States. I've seen what you have to go through. I cannot imagine it. Anything I do pales in comparison to the adversity, the challenge, the stress, the pain, the frustration of being away from your wife and your family, all the while still getting up there and doing your job because you know other people need inspiration more than you do right in that moment.

That Charlotte crowd arrived in the rain and had dreamed of seeing Barack Obama because he spoke to their hope. Yet they would have understood that because his grandmother had died, he didn't feel like giving a speech and would rather just go and rest one night or return to Hawaii and spend time with his family and bury his grandmother. He put their needs ahead of his own. As he gave that rally in Charlotte in the rain, he cried. He cried but he kept going. And for me, that's the biggest inspiration, to keep going when times are hardest, when you're tired or emotional or grieving.

> I knew he was hurting. I could see the exhaustion in his face. I noticed the slight droop of his tired eyes. But what I saw more than anything else was a man destined to persevere through whatever adversity came at him.

All presidents, all leaders, will face adversity. They face it every day. But instead of being beaten down by adversity and giving up, they are inspired to push forward. When others see strength in the face of difficult times, they are inspired by such leadership, and the best leaders inspire others to action. That kind of inspiration creates lasting impact.

CHAPTER 3
SERVE

A gift from the skies, to be recognized. I'm keeping
my eyes on the people. That's the prize.

—Common, "The People"

G rowing up, I was familiar with John F. Kennedy's best-known words from his inauguration speech: "Ask not what your country can do for you; ask what you can do for your country." But I remember those words from a sample of that speech that opens the rap song "Wordz of Wisdom" by 3rd Bass. The famous words from Kennedy's inauguration address epitomize a call to service. They were intended to challenge a generation on how they saw their role in a democracy; they were a call for ordinary citizens to serve, paralleling what we should ask of all leaders: to recognize that their responsibility is to the people and to the organizations they lead. President Kennedy's words made sense to me because I had grown up in an environment of service, watching my family: my dad's career of service to the nation in the navy, my mom's service to students and their families as a teacher and principal, and my aunt's long days of serving patients as a nurse and "days-off" helping my mom raise my brothers and me because my dad was out at sea. A call to service was what I had heard from Chuck D.

In 2014 I was blessed with the opportunity to be a resident fellow at the Institute of Politics at the Kennedy School of Government at Harvard. The Institute of Politics was started by Jackie Kennedy after her husband's assassination because she wanted to continue his legacy by creating an unending pipeline of people in higher education committed to service. Living in Cambridge, Massachusetts, I spent days upon days in the Kennedy Presidential Library, learning about his presidency and his own commitment to service. Walking through his life, if you will, by studying in the museum dedicated to him, I followed his path of public service, including his time in the navy and his campaign for public office. I was struck that there was so much thoughtfulness about his role as a leader, that he was never cavalier about anything in his life. All his actions and decisions were directed, purposed, and his life was all about service. And one of my most striking realizations about John F. Kennedy is that he didn't have to do any of these things. His grandfather and father had made so much money and had so much influence that John, his brothers and sisters and even their children could have chosen to never work.[7] But they made the choice to serve. That is the ultimate message about the role of really

> **That is the ultimate message about the role of really meaningful leadership. You must make a choice.**

---

7   Carl O'Donnell, "How the $1 Billion Kennedy Family Fortune Defies Death and Taxes," Forbes, last modified July 8, 2014. https://www.forbes.com/sites/carlo-donnell/2014/07/08/how-the-1-billion-kennedy-family-fortune-defies-death-and-taxes-3/#6b096ee04e4a.

meaningful leadership. You must make a choice. You must make a conscious effort. That effort includes seeing the nature of leadership in a new light.

The highest mark for any leaders is recognizing that their job is to serve first and lead second. Service means having a deep commitment to helping others achieve their goals and dreams even if your own goals become secondary. When you have this mind-set of service to others, you gain the greatest amount of influence. The most influential leaders in any organization are always the leaders who commit to service, in part because those they serve will be loyal to them and because the organization thrives under such a mind-set.

Some leaders like to think they need to manage people. You don't need to manage people. You need to lead people. The term *manage*, in my definition, is about restriction. It's about minimalization. It's about control. But leadership is about elevation. It's about expansion. It's about innovation.

I could see Kennedy's example

The highest mark for any leaders is recognizing that their job is to serve first and lead second.

in my paternal grandfather. Unlike Kennedy, he was a man who had to work hard for every dime he earned, but what he did in the neighborhood I saw as servant leadership. He was a community leader in the Cavalier Manor neighborhood of Portsmouth, Virginia, that neighborhood Nathan McCall wrote about where my father grew up. My grandfather volunteered his time to the people of the neighborhood throughout his adult life, including in the 1980s when it had fallen into really hard times. He may not have served on any boards or led a nonprofit, but he was larger than life in the neighborhood. People in Cavalier Manor always called him by his nickname,

Peter Gunn. To this day, when my brother Jamal does community work in Portsmouth and tells people his last name is Gunn, people ask if he is related to Peter Gunn even though my grandfather died several years ago. There wasn't a person who didn't know who Peter Gunn was because of how he would go around helping people. His day job was that of a shipyard electrician. That was his skill, his expertise. And when he left the shipyard, he used his skill to help others with things they couldn't do on their own. So he spent his time away from his paying job doing electrical work, putting up ceiling fans, replacing people's air conditioning units, and so on. Every weekend he did that. And he never asked for a dime. He felt it was his job to serve, and that made him an influential member of his community. As my grandfather did, good leaders lead by example.

Kennedy's example and my grandfather's example demonstrate a central component of leadership: committing to something bigger than you. Leading is not about your self-preservation or gaining personal wealth or personal resources; it's about what you can do for other people. Their examples correspond to my belief that everyone has something to contribute, and the best leaders are the ones who figure out the best contributions those they serve can make. One of the first principles of service is that a leader has to look for the potential in people. You've got to be one of those folks who are able to analyze what others may have to contribute to the team or to their own success. These can be large contributions or small ones. It doesn't matter. When I was working for President Obama's campaign, as the political director, we had a group of older volunteers who felt they weren't mobile enough or

Leadership is about elevation. It's about expansion. It's about innovation.

didn't possess the high energy of some of us leading the campaign. Stacey Brayboy was the state director and Jeremy Bird was the field director, and together we asked these women to cook for the staff because we never took time to break away from the campaign to eat. The next thing I knew was that we had home-cooked meals in the campaign office every day. These women who worried that they didn't have anything to contribute were not only contributing but providing the most meaningful thing to everyone in the office because you can't keep up the stamina needed for a presidential campaign without nourishment.

Second, service is about teaching. The most effective leaders teach more than they lead. That was a lesson I learned immediately out of college because Lenora Bush

The most effective leaders teach more than they lead.

Reese made it clear that I should never be afraid to ask her a question, and she never thought it was a problem to take time to answer my questions or to teach me the nuances of policy or demonstrate ways to reach out into the community. She taught me to read the editorial pages of the newspapers, specifically the letters to the editor, for by doing so, I quickly learned what was on the minds of community members and knew where to start a conversation. She provided me opportunities to learn, even going so far as to encourage me to apply for participation in the Community Change Agents Project, a national leadership development program funded by the Kellogg Foundation. Because of her support, my application was accepted and there I was at twenty-four years old learning from and alongside people who had directed nonprofits for twenty or thirty years. She was constantly teaching me and providing me resources to learn from.

When I think of Lenora, I also think about Arlene Andrews, a professor of social work at the University of South Carolina, whom I first met in 1997 while doing work for a small, child advocacy organization and I later worked for her when I was in graduate school. She had a tremendous amount of expertise, but she never came in the room and beat you over the head with it. I don't know anyone who has ever called her "Dr. Andrews"; they called her "Arlene" because even though she was the smartest person in the room, she never behaved that way. Instead, she literally gave as much as she possibly could to her teams.

Third, the best leaders build people up and don't tear them down. You tell people what they're doing well and show them what they need to do better, but you do it in a way that helps them improve. Lenora was that kind of leader. She built people up. Barack Obama builds people up. The best leaders, the greatest leaders, build people up. John F. Kennedy showed people their potential and then helped them to realize it. When you think of his role in the space race, he helped the whole country believe that we could do something that nobody thought was possible. When you build people up, you inspire them, and then you give them the tools they need to be successful. When they thrive, the entire organization thrives.

The best leaders build people up and don't tear them down.

Nowhere are these models of servant leaders more important than in health care. Those who are leaders in the American health care system know it is a system in crisis. It is broken in the ways that all the personal care professions are broken: from stress and burnout. These are not the things the public hears about or that become the center of political discussion. It's palpable to me that there's so much pressure on people in health care. There's regulatory pressure. There's financial pressure. There's competitive pressure. There's consumer pressure. These are very real problems, often overwhelming ones, yet the real crisis is that the people inside health care systems, all those who have dedicated their lives to healing others, are in desperate need of leaders to serve them. I work at an academic medical center and I can tell you that right now, we are failing our health care workforce. Our own people are sick. They are tired, overworked, unhealthy, and psychologically overwhelmed. Every day they face pressure to produce at the highest level possible without any regard to their own health. Much of the fault lies in a broken foundation of leadership in health care.

I once heard a hospital executive suggest that the average patient who comes into a hospital for care could have contact with 200 care team members during his or her stay. That's not just contact with nurses and doctors but also all the others who make a hospital function and help patients receive care: the registration staff, the patient care technician, the dietician, the phlebotomist, the physical therapist, the parking attendant. Think of those who clean patients' rooms or those who serve meals, the ones who cook those meals or those who provide security so that the patients' stay is safe. All 200 of them are serving those patients. Each one of these roles comes with significant amount of stress.[8] It only takes one scratch below the surface to see how difficult life is for people who work in health care, difficulties evidenced from a simple review of turnover and burnout rates.[9]

---

8   "Health Care Workers May Be the Nation's Most Stressed
     Employees," Advisory Board, last modified February 13,
     2014, https://www.advisory.com/daily-briefing/2014/02/13/
     health-care-workers-may-be-the-nations-most-stressed-employees.
9   "Hospitals Face Unprecedented Turnover, Attrition Rates: 4 Survey Findings,"
     Becker's Hospital Review, last modified May 11, 2017, https://www.beckershos-

Unfortunately, the foundations of leadership in health care have been wrong-minded from their outset. Despite those 200 care worker contacts serving a patient during their stay in a hospital, the health care industry does not see itself as a service industry. It never has. In health care, we have the highest level of competency and knowledge about the most complex and most difficult things there are: medical care. What is more complex than human anatomy and the human body? The entire health care model, from its inception, was built on solving problems, on fixing things that were broken, or using expertise to solve problems. Over the history of medical advancement, we've become very smart about solving problems in the complexity of the body, we've become adept at creating medical solutions, but we don't see ourselves as serving people. If you don't see yourself as a service industry, with the responsibility to serve your patients, then you breed an environment where patient focus disappears and organizational problems spiral out of control.

Much of the environment in health care stems from the unconscious application of the "God complex."[10] Because of the expertise mastered by doctors, we have created the perception that, internally and externally, the healers have all the power in their hands. They have all the control. They have the ability to make the impossible possible. That mind-set is not only present among doctors; it's how hospitals also tend to think: the whole framework around innovation and transforming health care and bringing the newest technology into the operating room and using this new cool tool that solves this

---

pitalreview.com/human-capital-and-risk/hospitals-face-unprecedented-turnover-attrition-rates-4-survey-findings.html.

10   Maureen Dowd, "Decoding the God Complex," *The New York Times*, September 27, 2011, https://www.nytimes.com/2011/09/28/opinion/dowd-decoding-the-god-complex.html.

one problem is about fixing things that are broken and solving problems. But what gets lost in that mind-set is serving people.

Too often we enter the examination room with the mind-set that we're smarter than the patient. Doctors have devoted their lives to becoming medical experts, but they must also acknowledge that the patient knows more about what has happened to their bodies and their lives than the doctor could ever understand. If I've lived to be forty-five years old, you can bet I know more about what I've done in my life and to my body than any doctor I meet tomorrow or the next day or the day after. And so, do physicians show deference for my personal expertise about my body and what I put in it and what I'm concerned about or what I feel?

> Because of the expertise mastered by doctors, we have created the perception that, internally and externally, the healers have all the power in their hands. They have all the control. They have the ability to make the impossible possible

Can they stop just trying to fix it based upon the last nine patients they saw, who came in with the same symptoms?

We must turn to the collective expertise in the room and that must include the expertise of the patient. We don't have to disregard the expertise of those working in the health care industry; we just have to augment it and deindustrialize it. It is up to health care leaders to create the environment where that is the case. I often think about a story told by my former colleague Dr. Rick Wild, who is the chief medical officer at the Centers for Medicare and Medicaid Services in Atlanta. When, as a physician in Boston, he finished his residency in emergency medicine and encountered his very first emergency room patient, Dr. Wild had an entire team of nursing leaders around him. Yet they all deferred to him on what to do to save the patient's life because the system they worked in constantly reinforced the belief that no one knows more than the doctor. Rick recognized immediately that many of these nurse practitioners and ER staff had been in this emergency room for ten years before he got there, but they all looked to him as the expert. He understood that leaders cannot discount the knowledge and experience of their team. Just think about the toxicity of a leadership environment where you have people who have tremendous amounts of expertise and experience, who've been there longer than you have, and now they have to take a backseat to you, despite your inexperience in that particular environment, merely because you have the title of leader, or physician. Imagine when the experienced physician has to make decisions by factoring in administrative policy or cost or scheduling or availability of facilities or technologies. Imagine you are a patient, scared, likely alone, in pain, confused by the events that have placed you in the alien environment of an emergency room. Do you want to be seen as a set of problems in need of solution or as a person in need of some help? Now imagine that the medical team attending to you are in hour ten of a twelve-hour shift that has been filled with other patients in crisis. The patient and the medical staff alike face many of these scenarios because of a lack of effective leadership. Yet such a hierarchical vision of who controls knowledge and decision making is at the root of the culture of health care.

> **Leaders cannot discount the knowledge and experience of their team.**

If you study the findings of employee engagement surveys in health care settings, the lowest scores consistently come from those in nursing and those in support services: the people who clean the rooms, the people who cook the food, the people who take care of the equipment, the facilities staff who take care of the building, and so on. Those scores are all in the toilet in terms of job satisfaction or

Do you want to be seen as a set of problems in need of solution or as a person in need of some help?

in terms of engagement in regard to feelings of worth and perceptions of having value. Part of redirecting your focus from a leadership focus to a patient focus also means redirecting your focus to the people you lead.

Among my many duties at the Medical University of South Carolina (MUSC), I have the great privilege of supporting hospital chaplains. I have learned from them how much counseling they need to do with the medical team. The toughest part of the job for them are not about the patients who died or the patients who just received news that their cancer is terminal; the toughest conversation for chaplains and social workers is to talk to a colleague about all of the personal challenges that they're going through. Health care workers take very little time for themselves or their emotions or their reactions to impossible circumstances because they have this constant burden of responsibility to care for others. Just as Lenora Bush Reese saw things, you, as a leader, must not only see the potential in people but also build people up, show them what their value is, show them what their worth is, and affirm that worth. You must let them know that they're the most important part of the machine, the most critical part of the entire operation.

You must be willing to stand side by side with the people you lead. This will help you to build relationships with your team members. It also helps you to see their jobs, and yours, from their perspective. Cultivating these relationships will increase the respect and support you get from your team. Serving those you lead will also cause you to gain a better understanding of how you can improve their lives. Using your leadership skills to improve the lives of others is how you yield the greatest amount of influence. Doing so should be your most critical responsibility.

> **You must be willing to stand side by side with the people you lead.**

Among the health care leaders I have been inspired by is Don Berwick. He helped found the Institute for Healthcare Improvement. We met when we were both at Health and Human Services and he was the administrator of the Centers for Medicare and Medicaid Services. Whether Don was focused on reducing hospital-acquired conditions—this scourge of secondary infections and other conditions patients often get during a hospital stay—or creating overall quality improvement at reduced costs, he placed people's attention not on him, not on the system, not on the process, but on the people whom we're all supposed to help. He believes, first and foremost, that we all have to be loyal to the mission of focusing on those we're here to serve. The second thing he believes is having people focused on quality improvement. He ascribes to the belief that in everything you do, you've got to inspect what you expect. If you expect top-notch, quality outcomes, you have to inspect what you're doing, and you have to create a repetitive process to review your procedures. And when we make mistakes, when things go wrong, he asks how we look at the root cause, how we change what we're doing so we don't have those negative outcomes. That is the mind-set of a service-focused leader.

A vision like that of Don Berwick or Lenora Bush Reese or Arlene Andrews rises out of experience. They rose to positions of leadership because of that experience of gathering knowledge piece by piece by being on the ground and learning from it. Then they seek out the expertise of those around them. In health care, the tradition of "rounding," the time-honored tradition of performing the activities of clinical care at the patient's bedside and providing medical instruction to nurses and doctors, dates back to the middle of the seventeenth century.[11] Despite a precipitous decline in the use of bedside teaching and an ever greater reliance on technology in its place, rounding remains a best practice in medicine. But we have to round for the right reasons; we must do it with intention. And when rounding, we must remember to ask our team members, "What do you need?" The idea of rounding as a direct opportunity to check in with your staff and listen to their needs applies as much in other settings as it does in health care. How can leaders possibly know what the people they lead are experiencing if they themselves are not regularly and intentionally meeting one-on-one with their people?

If you're a nursing manager, how do you make sure you're taking care of your people in the stressful environment of a hospital if you don't round? If you are a project manager, how can you know what obstacles your team members face if you don't check in with them directly? As leaders, we cannot get so caught up in budgets or sched-

---

11   Jed D. Gonzalo, Cynthia H. Chuano, Grace Huang, and Christopher Smith, "The Return of Bedside Rounds: An Educational Intervention," *Journal of General Internal Medicine,* no. 8 (August 25, 2010): 792–798, https://doi.org/10.1007/s11606-010-1344-7.

uling or organizational politics that we fail to see the experience of the people whom we lead. When nursing leaders, particularly the directors, aren't at the bedside, they lose touch with what it means to take care of the patient. It is not that they have forgotten, but the demands of other duties mean they don't often put themselves in proximity to the nurses who are directly working with the patients. By losing this direct nurse and patient contact, they create a vicious cycle. They focus more on budgets and finance, they focus more on management, they focus more on sending e-mails and telling people what they should and should not do, but they forget much of what is happening on the floor. Caring for patients has grown distant from decision making. As leaders, we must spend time on the frontline. A good prescription for any leader at any level is to get as close to the patients and the frontline staff as possible. By being directly involved, we can then not only encourage and empower our staff but also help them develop the skills they need to succeed and we can see when they or our systems are ailing.

We have to serve our patients and customers. We have to attend to our staff members. We must invest in them. They all need each other. As a leader you can point out the common goal, but in order for people to agree to this common goal, they have to see themselves in it. To borrow from a quotation ascribed to Gandhi, leaders have to be the change they want to see in the world. You've got to live it. You've got to live it every day. That is the true nature of service.

PRESIDENTIAL PRINCIPLE NUMBER TWO
Answer the Call to Serve

Much like President Kennedy, Barack Obama had no reason to choose a life of service although he did not come from a family of wealth and power. The man has two Ivy League degrees. Because he was smart and driven from a young age, he grew up valuing education and earned an undergraduate degree from Columbia and a law degree from Harvard. It would take but the most cursory research to identify that many who graduate with two Ivy League degrees, particularly one from Harvard Law School, could probably make as much money as they want. They could, literally, make a decision to work hard in their career and take care of their family and make enough money to pass that wealth on to two or three generations. But Barack Obama did not choose that path. Instead, he made a decision very early on in his life that he wanted to serve.

After he finished his undergraduate degree, he went to Chicago, a place where he had never lived and didn't have any family. He went to work on the south side helping low-income families start programs that improved the quality of their lives, focusing on job placement and job training. For three years he walked Chicago's streets, knocked on doors, organized meetings in churches and schools and town halls and parks. He attended block parties and church socials and spent time in barber shops listening to people and getting to know their lives and their needs.

Then he decided he could help people better if he were a lawyer. And so he made the decision to attend law school, after which he went right back to the same Chicago neighborhoods where he had learned the principles of community organizing to run a voter registration program focused on people of color.

While in law school, he worked as an associate at the famous law firm of Sidley and Austin, where he met his future wife, Michelle. She further fueled his belief in service, for after her time at Sidley and Austin, she held public sector positions in Chicago city government and then became the executive director of the Chicago office of Public Allies, an organization focused on developing programs to help young and underserved people do greater things. Looking at her example, is it little wonder than that her husband, a graduate of Harvard Law School and Columbia, returned to Chicago to drive around the projects carrying clipboards and registering people to vote, trying to empower them?

Once Obama passed the bar and became a lawyer, he didn't work with classmates in New York firms or join a big corporate law firm in downtown Chicago, overlooking Lake Michigan and charging $600 per billable hour. He didn't become a permanent fixture at Sidney and Austin. He chose to work for a small public interest firm. He chose to serve.

He then made the decision to become further involved in public service by representing people politically. First running for the state senate and then for the US Senate, precisely because he saw his impact could be greater. Eventually, he made the ultimate commitment to service: he knowingly chose to give up himself, his time, and his energy and put himself, his past, and his family through the public spectacle and public scrutiny of a presidential campaign. Sane people don't put themselves through that if they're seeking fame or power or fortune. He chose to serve.

All along his path his intent was about doing the most good for the most people at every level, and you don't get a more powerful example of where serving others can take you than by committing yourself to attaining the highest office in the land. For Barack Obama, the presidency meant taking a position from which he would be able to do the most good for the most people. That's why, once he achieved the presidency, he made the decision to tackle something that no other president before him could ever do: health care. Because of his leadership, twenty million people have access to health coverage today who didn't have it before, and the uninsured rate in America is lower than it's ever been in the history of insurance. He chose to take on a policy issue most saw as impossible. He chose it as his focus because he saw it as the arena that would have the greatest impact on people's lives. There was a problem to solve, certainly, but he approached the solution by staying focused on serving people's needs. His commitment to people resulted in a monumental presidential impact.

Yet when I think of President Obama, I focus on that young man, just out of college, who chose to spend his formative years on the south side of Chicago helping poor families when he didn't have to. I can't think of a more defining example of service.

This principle of leadership—the choice to serve—is the simplest of all the ideas in this book. But the act of doing so, the actual commitment to see yourself as a servant to others, is the most difficult of all. The rest of the principles we can learn from presidential leaders are things we can digest and put to use. To choose to serve must come from within.

PART II

EMPOWERMENT

The purpose of power is to be distributed, not hoarded, but only secure leaders are able to give their power away.

—John C. Maxwell

CHAPTER 4
THE MOMENT OF TRUTH

Cultivate, multiply, motivate, or else we'll die.
You know I be the master of the who, what, where and why.

—Gang Starr, "Moment of Truth"

W hen you are seventeen, sometimes your first steps into positions of leadership are a bit audacious—in my case, maybe even a bit arrogant. Largely, it's about being naïve about how the world works. Looking back, it's a simple point, really: you have to learn how to become a leader.

Before entering my senior year, my football coach, Ralph Gahagan, retired. The year before, Coach Gahagan had asked to meet with my mom and me. He laid a little flipbook out on his desk, titled, *NCAA College Admissions*. He said, "Mrs. Gunn, I want to tell you that your son is incredibly talented, and from what I've seen, he could go to college and play football. He's athletic, he's fast, and he's smart." Then he told us what kind of grades I needed to meet NCAA requirements. I didn't have a clue about college. Everybody else at Kempsville High School was going, I just never thought about it. So, when Coach Gahagan, this man who helped me see I could have a future, announced he was going to retire at the end of my junior year, I was devastated. He showed me he believed in me and in my abilities even though I played tight end and seldom caught the ball, because Gahagan believed in smash-mouth football; we threw two passes a game on a good night.

With his announcement, I had two things going through my mind. One, I had no idea if my new coach would share Coach Gahagan's belief. I was worried that if I didn't have a coach who vouched for me with the college recruiters, I wouldn't get a scholarship. And two, because I was a tight end, I really wanted to catch the ball. I hoped the new coach would give me a chance to prove myself as a receiver.

I had to prove it to myself first. The truth is I couldn't catch. I was tall and built like a tight end, but I served our running game better than I did being a threat as a receiver. That summer I would go to my high school and have my brother Cherone throw me the ball. I would stand behind the goal posts with my arms around them so I couldn't see where the ball was coming from until it got close to me or I'd have Cherone throw tennis balls and catch them with one hand as I was running routes.

I read in the newspaper the date the new coach was scheduled to meet the principal, so I sat in the parking lot and waited for him, whoever he was. I walked up to him and said, "You don't know me, but my name is Anton Gunn and I play football. You're going to be my coach, and I want you to throw me the ball because I'm going to go to college and play, and I can't do it without a good football team." I guess I was no longer the shy kid from middle school. He couldn't believe that I had approached him but seemed impressed that I was willing to do so.

His name was Jackie Wisman. When the season started, Coach Wisman named me cocaptain. If Coach Wisman was going to put faith in me as a team captain, I was going to do all I could to lead by example. I committed myself to never being second in any drill. That idea of leading by example has stayed with me and remains something I demand of myself and of all who lead.

I also had teammates I looked up to as leaders and didn't want to let down. One was Travis Hunter. He was the kind of leader I wanted to be. You didn't want to disappoint him because you could tell he believed in you, and so you wanted to perform because Travis was going to perform. Travis and other guys on that team were what I now call "impact players," the kind of players who always push themselves to perform at a high level. Everybody around them gets better because of the work ethic, the energy, the focus, the commitment, and the passion they demonstrate. That was the kind of leader I wanted to be.

Travis and other guys on that team were what I now call "impact players," the kind of players who always push themselves to perform at a high level. Everybody around them gets better because of the work ethic, the energy, the focus, the commitment, and the passion they demonstrate. That was the kind of leader I wanted to be.

I worked hard on the field and off. I took summer school classes in the subjects such as math, which I struggled with to bring my grades up and I performed well in classes such as English and history, in which I had always done well. I led by example in practices and tried to be a good teammate. As Coach Gahagan had promised, the college recruitment letters began to pour in. And as Coach Wisman had promised, he formed an offense that would allow me to catch the ball. But the very first game of my senior year, I injured my ankle and had to miss the next three games. I kept my head high and tried to motivate my teammates. And in the fourth game of the season, when I came back to the team after my injury, my coaches' belief in me and my belief in myself paid off. Literally, on the last play of the game, Coach Wisman called a play for me to get the ball, and I caught an eighteen-yard pass that I ran in fifty-nine yards for a touchdown. In my senior season, I averaged 24.9 yards per catch. I was getting college coaches' interest because I was kind of a dichotomy since I was six feet five inches tall and weighed 225 pounds, but I ran a 4.61 forty, so linebackers had a hard time catching me and defensive backs couldn't tackle me.

I had someone ask me one time, "What's the moment when you felt you were your best self?" My answer is that summer before my senior football season. I was working on my own to improve myself. I didn't have anybody to make me do the work. I've suffered sometimes from not wanting to do things I'm supposed to do, but at this moment I was doing it on my own, and I was preparing for my future. I knew I could succeed because Coach Gahagan believed in me. I wanted Coach Wisman to know that I was going to be the leader that he and the team needed me to be. I wanted to show what I was capable of accomplishing. This is a leader's attitude.

My work didn't go unnoticed. The letters and brochures started to fill our mailbox, from UCLA, West Virginia, Michigan, Ohio State, Penn State, Stanford, Arizona, Purdue, Auburn, Kentucky, Florida, East Carolina, Virginia Tech, and Temple. I received serious interest from Tennessee and from Wisconsin, from schools in Texas and all over California. When the letters came in the mail, I would segregate them into two boxes. If I was interested, I kept the letters in my bedroom. If I wasn't, I put them in a box I gave to my baby brothers so they could open the envelopes and cut out the helmets or the footballs to make little posters. Coaches would come to my school and ask to get me out of class. I was so audacious that I would refuse to meet with them unless it was a school in which I was interested.

But then it became time for me to pick schools for the five official visits that are all the NCAA allows an athlete. I chose University of California Los Angeles (UCLA), Ohio State, Virginia Tech, Tennessee, and North Carolina State (NC State). My first official visit was to NC State, and both my parents were able to accompany me. I loved being on a college campus, and my dad was impressed. Then, roughly a week after that official visit, President George H. W. Bush formally asked Congress to authorize use of force to drive Iraq out of Kuwait in the Persian Gulf. My dad was called away to Operation Desert Storm. At the time, I thought I really wanted to go to UCLA, but once my dad was deployed, I couldn't imagine being so far from my mom if she needed my help, and with my dad gone, I thought my brothers needed a male role model. So, I reconfigured my list and eliminated every school that was more than six hours away by car with the exception of Ohio State.

Eventually, I narrowed my choices to NC State and the University of South Carolina. I couldn't make up my mind, so I did what any seventeen-year-old would do: I pulled out a sheet of paper, tore it into ten pieces, and wrote "NC State" on five and "South Carolina"

From that random decision began the rest of my life. I've lived a remarkable life, but it's not unique.

on five. I folded the pieces of paper, and put them in my Washington Redskins hat. I said, "I'm going to pull out five, and whichever school has the majority, that's where I'm going." I pulled out the first one. It read, "South Carolina." The second one read, "South Carolina." I started to get nervous because I really liked NC State, so I shook the hat some more. The third one read: "South Carolina." I picked up the phone, called Coach Brad Lawing, and told him I was committing to becoming a Gamecock.

> **We all share similar stories. What I can see now is that all leaders are fortified by their experiences, and those experiences help them to inspire, motivate, and relate to other people.**

From that random decision began the rest of my life. I've lived a remarkable life, but it's not unique. Who can't relate to making a flippant decision about where you want to go to college? Who can't relate to hanging out with the wrong crowd, or having a coach believe in you and wanting to prove that coach right? We all share similar stories. What I can see now is that all leaders are fortified by their experiences, and those experiences help them to inspire, motivate, and relate to other people.

When I accepted the scholarship to play for the Gamecocks, Coach Lawing promised me two things: even though he thought I would be a better fit on defense, he would honor my request to try me at tight end, and he promised I could wear the number eighty-seven, the number I had worn throughout high school. In return, I agreed that if I didn't cut the mustard in camp, I'd be happy to learn to become an outside linebacker. When I arrived to receive my gear, the jersey I was issued was number fifty-nine. No tight end has ever worn the number fifty-nine. Coach Lawing had reneged on what he promised me.

I was never given a chance to prove myself. I was so distraught by what I saw as betrayal that I struggled throughout my redshirt season. I had an eighty-nine mind-set, but I was in a fifty-nine environment. I questioned whether I had chosen the right college. I also had to face that there were twenty-four other players in my class and they were all so much more developed than I was as athletes. I certainly wasn't prepared for success playing defensive end, which was where Lawing moved me, and which meant putting hands down in the dirt and having to hit guards and tackles. I was 245 pounds, and I was asked to hit offensive linemen who were 300 pounds. My self-esteem was in the toilet.

> **I had an eighty-nine mind-set, but I was in a fifty-nine environment.**

Players either loved or hated Coach Lawing. He knew his stuff, but the tone and tenor of his engagement with players was not at all positive. He constantly screamed at players, and when he wasn't yelling, he would make jokes about players that were microaggressions. He likely believed that his tactics would make players better, but his approach was tearing me down. "Anton, you have a whole lotta potential as a football player," he used to say. "And you know what potential means? ... Potential means you ain't done shit yet." I have since come to believe that no one rises above low expectations. I believed the story he was telling me about myself.

I also believe that good leaders build people up. Coach Lawing's approach ruptured my mind-set about football. I never felt confident. My redshirt freshman year was no better. At the end of the year, when I attended my last one-on-one meeting, I had another audacious moment and was determined to tell Coach Lawing how I really felt. I told him he had promised my mother that he was going to treat me as if I were his son, that he had committed to being a good role model and father figure. I said, "Coach, I feel like you don't treat me like I'm a man. You don't treat me with respect." I became emotional and started crying. As I was pouring my heart out to him, Coach Lawing laughed in my face.

He laughed at me and then repeated one of his tired lines: "You're getting *better*, but you still ain't worth a shit." I had trusted this man. I believe that as a leader, you've got to be careful what you say to people. Life and death is in the power of the tongue. His words killed my spirit. A great leader does the opposite. A great leader needs to find the potential in people and help them realize that potential. A great leader speaks life into those they lead.

> **Life and death is in the power of the tongue. His words killed my spirit. A great leader does the opposite.**

I thought seriously about leaving South Carolina. I met with David Coryell, who managed the academic enrichment programs for athletes. "Anton," he said, "you remind me of a player that I had at University of Virginia. His name was Yusef Jackson. Yusef Jackson is Jesse Jackson's son. He was an Academic All-American football player, but he knew early on that he wasn't going pro, so he focused on his academics and how to improve himself as a leader." Coryell looked at me. "Anton, you are much more than a football player," he continued. "You can be a great leader." Coryell built me up.

I started taking summer classes. I did everything I could to immerse myself in the academic environment. That summer I moved in with two teammates, Jerry Inman and Ron Willis. Jerry and Ron were just as much students as they were athletes. They were intellectuals and motivated to succeed; before the age of thirty, they both were traders on Wall Street. They were also members of the same fraternity. Through Jerry and Ron, I began meeting other men who were leaders, including the president of the African American Student Association, the president of the college chapter of the NAACP, and the president of the student body, Steve Benjamin, who is now the mayor of Columbia, South Carolina. I was suddenly exposed to black men who were successful, academically focused, socially engaged, community involved—the kind of men I wanted to be. I joined Kappa Alpha Psi that next fall, and I moved to the offensive line. I got away from Coach Lawing.

I was suddenly exposed to black men who were successful, academically focused, socially engaged, community involved—the kind of men I wanted to be.

As a result, I had a great redshirt sophomore year academically, socially, and in football, but our team did not, and the coaches were fired. I didn't respond well to the newly hired position coaches, Mark Salva and Chuck Kelly. But I focused my attention elsewhere. Inspired by these student leaders who became my fraternity brothers, I became more active in social causes and began to see football and the abuse we suffered in a new light. I thought a lot about when

David Coryell had inspired me to see myself as more than a football player. I began keeping a journal on how much money USC was making. I thought about forming a player's union.

What many people don't realize is that coaches treat playing for them as a full-time job, and athletes who are academically serious have little time for anything including academics. You certainly don't have a way to make money, and I played long before student athletes were allowed stipends. Many African American athletes come from disadvantaged backgrounds. In my case, both of my parents had respected jobs, but we certainly weren't rich, and they had three other boys to care for. They could not afford to keep me in new clothes when I was, literally, outgrowing everything I owned. As a result, I resorted, basically, to living in what my teammate Keith Amos called "Shealy-wear," the word we came up with to describe the Gamecock sweats and T-shirts issued to us by our equipment manager, Jim Shealy. They were the only clothes that fit me.

Our schedules were packed, and if you had classes over the noon hour and were going to be on time for a 2:00 p.m. film session before practice, you likely didn't get lunch, and because practices often lasted until 7:00 p.m., by the time you showered or attended a mandatory study hall, the cafeteria was closed. I used to go around the dorms, bumming quarters off people I knew on the pretext I needed to call my girlfriend on the payphone, until I had accumulated $2.75, which allowed me to walk to Circle K gas station and buy two hot dogs, a bag of potato chips, and four cartons of Jungle Juice. The coaches wanted me to weigh at least 275 pounds but put us on such a demanding schedule, I was lucky if I got to eat. These were just some of the norms of being a student athlete. I would look around me at the stadium during a game and start to calculate the money football was bringing in on any Saturday, and I'd watch as coaches would be treated to family vacations when they signed a shoe contract, while I couldn't afford to buy deodorant or toothpaste. This Malcolm X moment would kick in and I thought, "I've been bamboozled. I'm being exploited and taken advantage of; this is like slavery."

The SEC had a Student Athlete Advisory Committee, but USC didn't have a representative on it because we did not have its equivalent on our campus, so I became the founder of the University of South Carolina Student Athlete Advisory Committee. I got the swim team involved, the tennis team—any of a number of non-revenue-generating sports—and they began speaking out about the need for representation and about the unfair treatment they suffered. A newspaper story appeared, quoting me as saying, "Athletes are slaves of the 90s."[12] A similar story about my activism had already appeared in *The Chronicle of Higher Education* the year before.[13]

> This Malcolm X moment would kick in and I thought, "I've been bamboozled. I'm being exploited and taken advantage of; this is like slavery."

Meanwhile, the summer before the season started, our offensive line coach, Chuck Kelly, told all of his players that we had to stay in Columbia and practice. I wanted to pursue an internship back home in Virginia. I needed work experience. Rather than support a decision that could help my long-term future, he said, "We're going to be a winning football team, and to do that, all of you have to stay here."

12   David Newton, "Sports, Studies Devour Time," *The State*, June 26, 1994, C1.

13   Debra E. Blum, "Series of locker-room revolts has some wondering about the clout of athletes," *The Chronicle of Higher Education* 39, no. 23 (February 10, 1993): A35.

The coaches forced us to lift weights at 6:00 a.m. every weekday. On Saturdays, they gave us a break, and they allowed us to work out at 7:00 a.m. Then, at the hottest point in the day, we were required to come back and run a mile and a half. Six days a week.

A reporter from the *Greenville News* wrote a story about the offensive line and how we demonstrated such great commitment by staying all summer to work out together.[14] In preparation for the reporter's presence, our coaches, basically, told us, "Make it clear you are here because you want to be." I felt compromised and pressed into lying. Dave Didion, the NCAA compliance officer for the university, smelled something fishy and challenged the coaches on our "volunteering." He demanded an opportunity to interview the players. Our coaches met with us and said, without much subtlety, if we didn't put the right spin on our summer activities, the program could be in violation of NCAA rules and could be disqualified from participating in bowl games. Some of the seniors had experienced little team success but felt that with a new head coach, Brad Scott, who had been part of a national title staff at Florida State, they had a legitimate chance to play in a bowl game. To give our teammates that chance, we all told Didion, "We all chose to stay because we want to get better," but it was not true for me.

That was enough to make me want out of the program, and out of the game entirely, so when I recognized that I had enough credits to allow me to graduate early—in three and a half years—I was determined to do so. I was a history major, which required me to complete a senior thesis, for which the necessary class was offered on Tuesdays and Thursdays at 2:30 p.m. That meant that I would have to be at least an hour late for practice on those days. My coaches gave me hell for it. I remember one day when I arrived, Coach Kelly blew his

---

14   "Early Birds Get Stronger and Better," *Greenville News*, Sunday, July 3, 1994, 33.

whistle and stopped drills. He said, "All right. Let's wait for the prima donna to show up. Here comes Anton Gunn, the man that's letting y'all down every Tuesday and Thursday because he can't show up to practice on time." It was a Coach Lawing experience all over again.

That made me more determined than ever to graduate in December and not return for my last year of eligibility. Graduation was on a Tuesday and the team was in two-a-days because we had qualified for a bowl game. I told my coach that I wouldn't be at practice.

"Well, why not?" he asked.

"Because I'm graduating in the morning," I said, still surprised that he didn't know his players at all.

"Well, okay. Be at afternoon practice," he said.

I explained that I had ten members of my family coming. "I want to celebrate with my family," I told him. "I'm graduating from college."

He replied. "You better be at practice. You can celebrate later."

I disagreed and didn't come to practice that day. I had three other teammates who made the same decision. At the end of Wednesday's practice, the coach asked the four of us to stand up. I thought he was about to tell everybody, "Look at these four guys, they graduated and they got their degree." But instead he said, "These four guys let you down because they didn't show up to practice yesterday, so they gotta run stadium stairs." Running

My coaches refused to celebrate my success. They made me run for it.

those stairs, I realized something I would never forget: leaders should celebrate the success of their people. My coaches refused to celebrate my success. They made me run for it.

I was a history major and wanted to teach high school, inspired by my high school teacher Eric Carlson, who empowered students and made them want to learn. But I didn't have the education courses that would allow me to receive teaching credentials, and because I felt so done with football, I wanted out. After we beat West Virginia in the Carquest Bowl—the first bowl game win in school history—I didn't want to go home to Virginia. So, it was back to Jerry and Ron's couch.

I started my job search from their couch. I didn't even own a suit. My teammate, James Flowers, had a suit he let me borrow. We were close in size, although I was a little taller. The only thing I owned was a pair of shoes, a birthday gift from my girlfriend. James also let me borrow his car. In two months, I interviewed no less than forty times wearing a suit with pants that were too short, arriving for interviews in a borrowed car. I felt inadequate and inept.

In interview after interview I heard some version of the same refrain: "Anton, you're very articulate. You seem smart. But the only thing on your resume is you played football and you got a degree. You have no work experience." The only job I could get was substitute teaching. It paid $7.35 an hour and I was lucky if I was asked to substitute two or three days a week. I became severely depressed. My life was in a downward spiral.

By the end of May, I couldn't take it anymore. I had an offer from an uncle who lived outside Washington, DC to live with him. He said I could help him move into the new house he was building and look for work with the help of my cousin, Tanya, who knew people on Capitol Hill. I interviewed another dozen times for house members and senators. I sent out blind resumes in response to *Wash-*

ington Post ads and ultimately, interviewed another thirty or forty times without result. I wasn't politically connected. I didn't even understand that you needed political connections to land a job in DC. I had moved from audacious to naïve, and, in my own opinion, pathetic.

Defeated, I called my mom and told her I needed to move home. While my mom made it clear that I was always welcome, there were lingering tensions; my dad was disappointed in my quitting football. Unable to get a job, I considered myself a failure.

> I had moved from audacious to naïve, and, in my own opinion, pathetic.

And now I had returned home to a dad who said, "You're going to have to live by my rules" as if I were still a teenager. My dad, among other men in my family, had been so proud of me going to college and playing football that I felt their disappointment as well, and on top of it, many of them held unrealistic perceptions that I had lost a chance to play professionally.

I signed on with Snelling Temporary Agency and accepted any work they could find, varying from short-term contracts tearing the fixtures out of an old store to clerical work. Eventually, I received a contract for several months for the Glasser and Glasser Law Firm to reorganize their file room and to work as a courier. There, I began to recognize bigger patterns in the people and the environment around me. I encountered cases that had impacted my own family, such as litigation with Owens Corning over its use of asbestos in ship building, something my grandfather had been exposed to, as attested to in a file I found bearing his name. Sometimes the locked pouches I carried to the bank contained checks totaling millions, which began to open my eyes not just to the amount of money attorneys were making but to the complexity of problems people were facing because of companies that ignored the interests of people.

I saw the same patterns within the firm. I worked alongside a woman named Jackie. Jackie had a little girl, Jasmine, and I would hear Jackie on her phone during her breaks complaining about how Jasmine's father never paid his child support. Listening to her, watching the flow of settlement money passing through the firm, and hearing of the cases of corporate greed and liability made me look at my life in new ways and see that despite seldom having enough money during my college years to wash my clothes or take my girl-friend to the movies, I had been a privileged college athlete receiving a valuable education. Jackie had no such opportunity. I heard her discuss the disparities and inequities present in the firm, the disre-spect she received from white peers, her inability to get ahead and create a different life for her daughter. She was like so many people who work hard and never get ahead.

I worked at Glasser and Glasser during the day and had a tele-marketing job at night, not feeling good about either. And I didn't have a family to support. How many people in America work a full-time job but have a part-time job on top of it because at the end of the month, they have more month left than they have money? The phrase that was to become so important to my life, serving "the least of these" began to ring in my head. I felt I was being awakened in a way that paralleled the stories told in the hip hop songs I loved.

Finally, with the help of a fraternity brother, Myron Terry, I found permanent, meaningful work. Myron was a lobbyist for a law firm in South Carolina, and many of the firm's clients were health care companies. Lenora Bush Reese was the executive director of a nonprofit called South Carolina Fair Share. Myron knew Lenora from lobbying at the statehouse and knew I was activist minded. When Lenora told him about an opening she had, Myron called me.

I decided I was going to get the job no matter what. I packed the used car my dad had surprised me with and drove straight to the job interview. It was June 1. Hot. I had on a white shirt and a tie and khaki pants and still didn't own a sports coat. Lenora had no reason to hire me, but she apparently saw something in me the resume could not demonstrate, and I received an offer of a position as a health care reform coordinator.

Lenora Bush Reese remains one of the most important mentors of my life. She took me under her wing, empowered me, and taught me the skills I needed to be a successful community

> The phrase that was to become so important to my life, serving "the least of these" began to ring in my head. I felt I was being awakened in a way that paralleled the stories told in the hip hop songs I loved.

organizer. I learned more working with her in the first few months than some people learn in a lifetime. My position was designed to advocate for changes in health care systems. Lenora taught me ways to meet people in the community and hear their concerns. My responsibility was to build power in the people I met, to teach them how to tell their stories, and help them learn to give voice to that power in ways that would make their elected officials listen. Working at Fair Share on a report about expanding the Children's Health Insurance Program was the first time I was quoted in a newspaper for something other than football. I felt I was doing work that made a difference.

During my time at Fair Share, I also met the woman who would become my wife. We met before I ever received my first paycheck. I was living temporarily with six fraternity brothers in a two-bedroom apartment—most of us spending parts of the summer sleeping on couches or on the floor. I had no money and there

Lenora Bush Reese remains one of the most important mentors of my life.

was no food in the house. One Saturday morning, my fraternity brother told me he knew two girls who were having a cookout. I told him, "Let's go because that's the only way I'm gonna eat." I didn't know a soul there. I walked in the house and I went right to the grill and fixed two hamburgers. When I went to the kitchen to get a drink, I saw another fraternity brother. I told him, "I don't even know whose house I'm in." He replied, "We're here for a birthday party." I asked, "Whose birthday is it?" A girl turned and said, "It's my birthday," and her name was Tiffany. I met my wife crashing a barbecue for her birthday. She remains the love of my life. Meeting Tiffany and starting a job after a year struggling through desperation and depression, I thought I was the luckiest man alive.

Lenora created one opportunity after another for me. Despite investing heavily in me through generously sharing her time and knowledge, when she saw opportunities for me to advance my career and increase my paycheck, she took action. At one point, she handed me a job announcement for another nonprofit. With her encouragement, I applied for the job, and when they called to check my references, Lenora told them I was making $25,000 and the only way they would get me is if they paid me $30,000. I was making $19,000. Lenora felt I was more valuable than what her budget allowed her to pay me.

Talk about empowering those around you. At the same time, she encouraged me to apply to join the Community Change Agents Project, a leadership development venture funded by the Kellogg Foundation through a grant to the Center for Community Change. And so, when I started the new job at the Alliance for South Carolina's Children, I had to get my new boss to write a letter to support my application for the project. I was successful in my application and the program took a deep dive into the civil rights movement in Selma. We learned Latino and Cuban-American politics in Miami, studied taxation without representation in DC, and came to understand activism from the leaders of the Black Panther Movement in the San Francisco Bay area. From the project, I not only significantly developed my leadership skills; I built a national network of other social justice leaders.

Under the leadership of John Niblock at the Alliance for South Carolina's Children, I learned to share his passion for children's health and early childhood education. When I was at Fair Share, we went to the statehouse to protest, lead marches, or to browbeat politicians, but John Niblock allowed me to register as a lobbyist. My new job required me to be in the state capitol working with legislators every week. The Alliance professionalized me, and I grew from a grassroots organizer to learn the orchestrations of legislation and how to lobby those in power.

Jennifer Henderson, who was the training director for the Change Agent Project, saw my effectiveness at being a social change agent and recognized I could not fulfill that role at the Alliance, so she encouraged me to apply for a position through the Center for Community Change (CCC). It was a position leading a demonstration project focused on helping poor youth who lived in public housing to graduate from high school and enter college or career preparatory programs. My boss at CCC, Othello Poulard, told me the dropout rate for kids who lived in public housing was 60 percent. It was imperative we made an impact. I was hired as the program coordinator for a two-million-dollar demonstration project. I didn't necessarily want to run a social service program, but it was an avenue into the organization that I felt was the Mecca of social change and social justice. Suddenly, I had thirty-eight people reporting to me, spread over five public housing projects. I felt inexperienced and wondered what I had signed up for. I came to CCC because I wanted to be around the great social change leaders who worked there and found myself running a social program. It was a quality program, meaningful to the kids it served and successful, with an 89 percent graduation rate, and yet I wondered if I belonged.

At the same time I was working for CCC, I read an article in the *Wall Street Journal* about a kid from Texas Tech, a hulking all-American football player who grew up in a poor, rural Texas town. He started for his four years at college but never made it pro because of injuries and ended up as a trailer park security guard back in the town where he grew up. Fred Kline was the reporter. The story touched a nerve in me and I reached out to Kline. He wrote a story titled "Looking Back, Ex-Lineman Takes College Sports to Task."[15] The story ran nationally, and in addition to being a kind of flashpoint in South Carolina, I received numerous calls and e-mails from athletes and their parents who shared similar stories to mine and who felt they had been taken advantage of by programs and disrespected by coaches.

---

15   Frederick C. Klein, "Looking Back, Ex-Lineman Takes College Sports to Task," *The Wall Street Journal*, September 25, 1998, W5.

Hearing such responses, I had an epiphany. I wasn't doing the work I was passionate about—hands-on work for social justice and creating change by fighting unfair systems. In the article I was quoted as saying, "When you're a so-called student-athlete, you have to fight the system to take advantage of the 'student' part." Not only did I believe that but it got me thinking about the education I still wanted and felt I needed.

> **I had an epiphany. I wasn't doing the work I was passionate about— hands-on work for social justice and creating change by fighting unfair systems.**

I was dating Tiffany and was in love with her. Now we were in a long-distance relationship. I knew I wanted to marry her and go back to South Carolina. I applied and was accepted to the College of Social Work at the University of South Carolina. On Easter weekend, on a visit to Tiffany's parents, I proposed to her.

We were married the following May. At the time, I was in the middle of my graduate program, finishing a field placement in a mental health center and working part-time as a house parent at an adolescent group home. My second field placement starting that fall was in the State General Assembly, interning with Gilda Cobb-Hunter, who ran a domestic violence agency in addition to her work as a legislator, and with Teresa Arnold, a master social worker who had recently left the Assembly for a position in the state Department of Social Services.

On October 12, 2000, my Thursday started as workdays always did, catching up with the news as I got ready for work. They reported a breaking story about a US Navy ship that had been bombed in the Middle East. That got my attention because my brother Cherone was on deployment somewhere in the Persian Gulf. Cherone had joined the navy in January and had completed technical training school just in time to attend our wedding in May. He had left on his first deployment on August 8. I had last heard from Cherone by e-mail on September 21, and he had told me they were going to be on maneuvers for three weeks and he wouldn't be able to correspond. I thought his ship would still be on maneuvers and not in a port, so this incident could not involve my brother.

I had been at my desk in the Office of Research for all of thirty minutes when my mom called. She asked if I had heard about the explosion and told me, "That was Cherone's ship. They were in port in some place called Yemen." Shocked, I told her not to worry, that we both knew if Cherone was in port, he wouldn't be on the ship because Cherone loved socializing and exploring; he would be out seeing the sights in the port city.

There were no televisions in the statehouse, and this was long before we all had news feeds on our phones, so I went down the block to my credit union, where I knew they had a TV. The newscast reported that there were four dead and thirteen missing and that the explosion occurred near the waterline. That gave me some relief again, because even if Cherone had been on board, he was a signalman, which meant he was stationed on the bridge, well away from where the explosion was reported. The navy wasn't telling the families much of anything. My mom didn't know much more than I did watching TV from the lobby of my credit union.

I spoke with my dad while he was driving from Washington, DC, to Norfolk and asked how it was possible that thirteen sailors were missing. He told me, "Son, sailors don't go missing on a navy ship. They are dead." After a check-in back at the statehouse with Gilda, I returned to the bank. That's where I was, still watching their

TV, when my dad called at 4:00 p.m. When I took the call, I heard him gasping and crying. "They killed my son. They killed Cherone. They killed your brother. They killed my son. They killed my son." My knees buckled.

Cherone was twenty-two. He'd been in the navy for ten months. The blast had been caused by two suicide terrorists who had packed a small fiberglass boat with C4 explosives, ripping a forty-foot by sixty-foot hole in the *Cole*. The blast was centered

When I took the call, I heard him gasping and crying. "They killed my son. They killed Cherone. They killed your brother.

on a mechanical room immediately below the ship's galley and was so violent it killed sailors lining up for lunch on the deck above.

Cherone had gone to lunch when he and others were dismissed from the bridge because it was too crowded with the harbor pilots on board and others attending to the needs of docking and refueling the ship. He had gotten his lunch and sat down with his friends but had forgotten his drink, so he rejoined the mess hall line. He was blown forty feet across the deck and into a doorway by the explosion. Other sailors attempted first aid, but he was already gone. He was one of the four sailors first listed as killed in the attack because, among the other thirteen, the remains were unidentifiable.

Cherone had joined the navy in order to gain experience that might help him fulfill his dream of becoming a cop. He had passed the written and physical tests for two different police departments, but they wouldn't hire him without a college degree. He had hoped that with experience in the navy he might be able to take some college credits, try to become a military policeman, and then be positioned to go into full-time law enforcement after serving his four years.

He was a friendly, easy-going kid who had done well in the service industry because he was so eager to help people. He had only begun to pursue a plan for his life when terrorists took his life.

When I heard the news of his death, I raced out of the bank and collapsed on the sidewalk, crying, as my father had. I screamed, "They killed my brother!" By the time Tiffany and I arrived at my parents' house, it was already filled with people who loved Cherone. I'd never seen my parents look as they did, frozen in absolute shock. The next several days were surreal. The flowers and cards and letters started arriving, as did the phone calls from politicians, including Jesse Jackson, Al Gore, and John Warner.

The following Sunday, Byron Pitts from the CBS Evening News called and asked if I would be open to an interview. I agreed. I'd done a number of radio interviews during my time at Fair Share and some television interviews when I was with the Alliance. Educated and articulate, I became a kind of de facto spokesperson for the families of the *Cole* victims. Almost immediately after the Pitts interview, I was asked to be on *Good Morning America* with Diane Sawyer, and the requests continued to pour in. While it was overwhelming to be thrust into the media spotlight in a time of personal tragedy, I thought it was a way to serve the families who were suffering and to honor Cherone. I set up conference calls with family members of those killed and tried to draw on the instruction I had gained for dealing with the media as part of the Community Change Agents curriculum to give advice about accepting interview requests to parents who had lost children on the *Cole*.

One piece of advice I gave consistently to others, and followed myself, was to demonstrate our sadness and emotion but not to express our anger. For in truth, we were angry: angry at the terrorists and angry at the bureaucracy that provided us so little information.

We were confused as to how a speedboat loaded with explosives could get within range of a billion-dollar naval ship. The navy largely stone-walled us. But there were plenty of nonmilitary sources, including journalists and navy retirees, who raised more questions. We learned that the previous year, the State Department had placed Yemen on a watch list of countries likely involved in state-sponsored terrorism. We learned that there were sixty-one security measures the captain should have directed the crew to undertake to protect a ship in a foreign port. Of those sixty-one measures, they didn't even complete thirty. As members of navy families, we were well used to a system where responsibility resides in a clear chain of command, and on a naval vessel, that chain of command starts and stops with its captain.

The commanding officer of the *USS Cole* at the time of the Yemen attack was Kirk Lippold. As most officers do, he came up through the US Naval Academy and pro-gressed through a series of promotions, but we heard rumors that his rapid rise was as much due to cronyism as to com-petency. We wanted answers, and Lippold and the rest of the navy were not **We wanted accountability and none was forthcoming.** providing them. We wanted accountability and none was forthcom-ing. We were grieving and the circumstances of my brother's death and the level of media interest made the personal nature of grief nearly impossible.

Instead, many of us who lost our loved ones to terrorists that day on board the *USS Cole* continued to press our government not just for more information about precisely what happened and whether proper procedures had been followed but also with an interest in ensuring similar attacks did not happen in the future. We continued to wait for a retaliatory attack against Al-Qaeda, which had claimed responsibility. When the US embassies in Kenya and Tanzania were bombed in 1998, we fired missiles into Afghanistan to try to get Osama bin Laden. We were very appreciative when President Clinton met with our families six days after the attack, but in his final months in office, his administration rushed through an investigation, and Clinton never retaliated against Al-Qaeda, frustrating some of his own counterterrorism advisors.[16]

> **If I had learned tremendous lessons about the impact of investing in the people around me from high school coaches, teachers, and employers such as Lenora Bush Reese to friends like my fraternity brothers, I also learned the hard lessons that had left me feeling betrayed by college coaches, naval officers, and the leaders of the bureaucracies that enabled such destructive leadership.**

Two senior investigators—one with the FBI and another with the Naval Criminal Investigative Task Force—later said there was compelling evidence that Al-Qaeda was responsible for the bombing. Two accomplices of the *Cole* bombers arrested by Yemeni security forces confessed their role and told investigators they were working for top Al-Qaeda operatives known to US intelligence. We could not understand why nothing was being done.

---

16   Michael Isikoff, "U.S. failure to retaliate for USS Cole attack rankled then—and now," NBCNews, last modified October 12, 2010, http://www.nbcnews.com/id/39622062/ns/us_news-security/t/us-failure-retaliate-uss-cole-attack-rankled-then-now/.

If there were any lingering doubts before Clinton left office, they were erased in the early days of Bush's presidency. In their first months in office, White House officials ignored repeated assertions from counterterrorism experts that bin Laden was using the bombing as a propaganda and recruitment tool.[17] President Bush continued to frustrate our families by refusing to meet with us. After the attacks of 9/11, his administration dropped us like a bad habit. I had an FBI Victim Witness Specialist assigned to me as a victim's specialist, and immediately after 9/11, she called and said she and all of her peers were being summoned to New York to support those families. It felt as if they had forgotten about the *USS Cole* and us. My mom and I came up with the phrase, "The only difference between 9/11 and 10/12 is one year, one month, and one day."

If I had learned tremendous lessons about the impact of investing in the people around me from high school coaches, teachers, and employers such as Lenora Bush Reese to friends like my fraternity brothers, I also learned the hard lessons that had left me feeling betrayed by college coaches, naval officers, and the leaders of the bureaucracies that enabled such destructive leadership. I learned that audacity could mean taking bold risks *and* it could mean treating others with disrespect, and I learned that when it came to leadership, these opposing meanings of audacity both existed. When we rise to positions of leadership, we face choices about the sort of leaders we wish to become.

---

17   Chris Whipple, "What the CIA knew before 9/11: New details," Politico, last modified November 14, 2015, https://www.politico.eu/article/ attacks-will-be-spectacular-cia-war-on-terror-bush-bin-laden/.

CHAPTER 5
ENGAGE

Crowd is captured, released at my permission.
Peep em, as I keep em eager to listen.

—Eric B. and Rakim, "Eager to Listen"

Because football was important in providing me some of the opportunities I've had in my life, it's hard not to turn to it for an analogy when talking about leadership and empowerment. Football can't be played without a team. Leaders can't accomplish everything by themselves, no more than a quarterback can catch his own passes or a tailback would have anywhere to run without an offensive line. A leader must build a team of people who are equipped to succeed. If service is the prerequisite of leadership, empowerment is its essence. Empowerment is about providing people with the tools, information, and the resources to make a difference.

First, you have to equip your people, provide them the equivalent of helmets, shoulder pads, and cleats—the specific equipment they need for the specific role they play. Then you have to give them a playbook. As a football player I needed that playbook to know what was expected of me. That information, combined with knowing what the rest of my team was supposed to do and how our opponent might react, gave me confidence that I could have success if I executed my responsibility. I was ready to engage in the game. In order for you to empower people, you must show them what engagement looks like. You have to help them to make a crucial decision: the decision to commit to something.

The highest functioning organizations are the ones that have the highest level of engagement from their employees. In health care, you not only get great patient satisfaction if your employees are engaged but you also benefit from higher revenue streams and better-quality outcomes. If you want to take care of your patients, take care of your people first. Taking care of your people starts with engagement. And if you engage your teams, they will feel empowered and equipped to make better

> **The highest functioning organizations are the ones that have the highest level of engagement from their employees.**

decisions that will improve the outcomes of everyone they serve. Then you can extend engagement beyond your health care team to patients. The equivalent can be true in any industry. In health care, we started to see better outcomes when we gave patients more tools and more information to manage their own health.

Part of building people up is giving them the tools they need to be successful. Among the tools good leaders provide are information, resources, decision-making power, and providing a support system that allows people to execute their responsibilities. The greatest part of a leader's impact is giving those under their leadership the means to have an impact themselves.

You can't empower anyone unless you first engage that person. And for starters, you can't effectively lead people you don't know. This is parallel to why I have shared a lot of my life story with you in this book. How can you understand why I have formed the presidential principles I now share if you don't understand who I am? In a similar fashion, you

Part of building people up is giving them the tools they need to be successful.

need to understand the people you lead. If you look at organizations that are the most successful at achieving outcomes, whether those are military units, hospital teams, business groups, or sports teams, the greatest organizations are the ones in which the team members have a relationship with one another and with their leaders. When I started my professional life at Fair Share, I found that one of the most powerful things about Lenora was that she would ask me questions about me and not about work. She always made it clear she was as interested in me as she was in the job I was doing, in part because doing so helped me do the job well.

You have to engage in practices that build relationships. Whenever I come into an organization, I try to get to know who my team members are. I start by recognizing that people love to share things about themselves that are important to them. Learning that I care about you as a person, not just about the role you're supposed to play in my organization, changes the dynamics of our relationship. And I don't just learn some facts about you and put them in a drawer. It's not enough to know employees' birthdays or how many dogs they have; it's how you reward people when you have the opportunity to reward them. If I have a team member who loves Italian food, when we finish a big project he was important in completing, I'm going to give him a twenty-five-dollar gift certificate to the best Italian restaurant in town. Can he really share a nice dinner with his partner for twenty-five bucks? No, but I want to acknowledge his contribution to the team, and he will remember that I was thoughtful enough to provide recognition. If I know I have a team member with a daughter on a high school basketball team and that team has made regionals and will play a Thursday afternoon game, I will suggest to that mom that she takes Thursday afternoon off, that I want her to be able to be supportive of her child. She knows I will expect her to make up that time. We've established a relationship of trust, so we both know she will make the time up.

> You can't empower anyone unless you first engage that person.

Ultimately, these are simple matters of rewards and recognition. People love to be validated; they need to be appreciated for what they do. When I worked at Health and Human Services, every Friday at our senior staff meeting, our boss, Paul Dioguardi, used to ask, "Who on your team did a great job this week?" We could all submit one name and he would decide who would receive the "game ball" that week. He had a whole collection of cheap toy balls, one for every season, and whatever the season was, he'd toss that ball to the person he had selected. They'd keep the ball on their desk for the week and bring it to the next Friday meeting. It was the simplest thing, but believe me, everyone competed to receive that game ball.

Another way I get to know my team members is that at every staff meeting I start with a question that will get them talking. I use such questions to get information out of my team members about what's important to them. I want to know what matters to them, what motivates them. I might ask, "If you could travel anywhere in the world at any point in history and have dinner with someone, who would you have dinner with and why?" Or "What's the worst thing a boss or supervisor has ever said to you?" Such opening questions can start important conversations that give me great insight into my team.

Such a mind-set also values the importance of one-on-one meetings. I cannot overstress the value of the engagement received from getting to know people at the individual level and hearing their perspectives on the organization. For me, such a practice goes back to what I learned from community organizing, and I don't ever depart from it. When I first arrived at MUSC, I possessed zero institutional knowledge, so in my first 100 days, I committed to completing 100 one-on-ones with the different people across the organizational chart. I actually did 141. When I conducted those 141 interviews, I listened before I spoke. I learned a bit about their lives and backgrounds and about their jobs and their experiences with the hospital. I wanted to know why they took the jobs they did and what motivated them to stay. I asked them what they thought was best about the organization and where they would like to see change. I listened intently. People expect a leader to take them to new heights, but they also expect a leader to be connected to the reality of where they have come from. Only at the end did I tell them briefly about myself. The last question I always asked was for them to tell me three things they thought I was there to do. No matter what role you play as a leader, you're given a job title; people who report to you know what your job title is, but the question is: what have you been hired to do?

Great leaders go beyond engaging those they lead; they share knowledge with them to ensure they will be successful. As a very young community organizer, Lenora empowered me by helping me develop the tools I would need to succeed, for not only did she believe in my success, she wanted those we served to be successful. She didn't stop at teaching me about health care; she taught me how to be a leader, how to engage more deeply with anyone I spoke with, and how to act with conviction. Nearly immediately upon hiring me, she poured out her address book for me. She introduced to me every friend and colleague she knew who could be helpful to me in doing the work she had hired me to do. She equipped me through experience and through her knowledge of what I needed to be effective. By engaging me, she taught me to engage others.

> **Great leaders go beyond engaging those they lead; they share knowledge with them to ensure they will be successful.**

Then we must give power to those we engage, just as Arlene Andrews did for me. Arlene was the director of the Institute for Families in Society. The newly elected governor had hired Arlene to research how to structure community and county-based partnerships focused on improving early childhood outcomes. Arlene asked me to put together the training program and the nonprofit research on how boards of directors should function. When I had completed the task, she said, "Now you're going to go around the state and present to these county partnerships." I was twenty-seven, and she showed me she believed in my abilities. Arlene was a masterful leader who built independent teams and empowered them to do what they knew how to do without micromanagement. Leaders such as Arlene and Lenora taught me more than what was required to be a better worker; they helped me become a better person and a future leader.

This kind of direct engagement with employees creates numerous opportunities for feedback. Every organization needs to learn directly from the frontline about what is working well and what is not. We must learn their needs and how we can help them. All this means we have to learn how to listen, which means hearing what is said *and* what is unsaid. Effective communication includes the words you say, the tone you use, and the body language that accompanies those words. Sometimes the body language doesn't match the words used, and we need to recognize that. Sometimes what is missing is the most important thing you need to hear. Active, intentional listening demands that you are aware of the things that are bigger than you and bigger than anyone's particular situation. When someone says something to you about your leadership or your organization, you must be able to hear all the issues within their comment. You should then take that information and translate it to the people within your organization to address the concerns at hand. By articulating the real problem, together you can address it. This ensures that you and your group can continue to pursue your purpose. By listening, you will keep people engaged and committed to the vision.

If we know our people and understand what motivates them, if we truly listen and receive feedback from them about how they can do their jobs better and make the organization stronger, then we have to equip them with a vision. We need to provide them **We need to provide them a roadmap for what success looks like.** a roadmap for what success looks like. We need to help them ask and answer the question: what's the impact of what we're doing? The leader is the one who can take each one of a myriad of perspectives within an organization and on a team and unify those perspectives around an end goal.

When you build teams of people who share a common purpose that you have been successful in articulating and you take the time to know your people as individuals with differing needs and divergent strengths, then you can better assess which roles each can excel in and best benefit the team. You must have an intimate understanding of people's skills, knowledge, and motivation if you are going to make certain you have the right people in the right positions.

The last thing that invites the most engagement is a leader's transparency. I don't ever want anyone on my team to find out what's going on in the organization from anyone other than me. That includes being transparent about our successes and our failures. By doing so, they come to trust that they won't be blindsided. They reciprocate by bringing me information that I might not know so I'm not blindsided. It becomes a positive, symbiotic relationship of sharing information. What employees want to know more than anything else from a boss is that they are respected and cared about as a person. Even if they never verbalize the questions, what they're thinking is, *Does the person I report to care about me? Is this person willing to help me to be successful?* When that care is genuine, teams can be empowered. Empowered people take accountability seriously, and empowered teams can accomplish tremendous things.

> **Empowered people take accountability seriously, and empowered teams can accomplish tremendous things.**

Engagement is ownership. Extreme ownership. As a leader, you have to own your responsibility, along with the opportunities, the successes, and the failures. In the end, people don't like to follow weakness or indifference or insecurity or people who are lukewarm. You've got to be hot or cold. People want to follow strength.

PRESIDENTIAL PRINCIPLE NUMBER THREE
Decide to Engage

My most direct experience with George W. Bush arises from a *lack* of direct experience. After my brother was killed aboard the *USS Cole*, my family, along with the other families of those killed, tried and tried to create opportunities for direct engagement with President Bush and his White House. Unfortunately, most of what we experienced was what I like to call antimatter: the opposite of engagement. As I have detailed, after 9/11, the families of the *Cole* victims felt brushed aside. We continued to have questions about the events that killed our brothers, sisters, daughters and sons and fathers and mothers, but we were not listened to, we were never engaged. And because leadership starts and stops at the top, we felt this was directly a product of George Bush's lack of engagement. Because there was no responsiveness, we felt our needs were never met and no trust could ever then be established.

In 2003 George Bush's appointee Attorney General John Ashcroft abruptly reached out to the families after two years of silence from the administration, asking us attend a press conference where they were going to indict two coconspirators in the attack on the *USS Cole*. To us, it felt like grandstanding. They were going to announce an indictment, not an arrest. They had no idea where the terrorists were. It was indictment in absentia. Then, in what felt like a slap in the face, we weren't allowed to be at the press conference. Instead we were held in a back room. When Ashcroft entered the meeting with us after the press conference, he had the attitude of someone thinking he was about the receive hugs and high fives. Instead, he encountered a group of victims who unloaded on him, demanding an opportunity to speak with the president. We wanted him to understand that our government was not being responsive to us and their indictment of coconspirators didn't make us feel any better. This was an administration that was fighting a war in Iraq when we knew that Al-Qaeda and Osama bin Laden were in Afghanistan.

Neither Ashcroft nor Bush engaged. Nor did their administrative leadership team follow any of the principles of engagement. In the absence of meeting with us, by demonstrating they had made no effort to understand us, our experience, or our frustrations, we felt disempowered and disenfranchised. I remember hearing some families say, "You know what? Our government is never going to do anything to help us and I could care less." They just drifted off the scene.

Mostly, all we really wanted was to be listened to. Some of us wanted someone to be held accountable. The analogy that I use to place our feelings in perspective is drawn from my mom's background. She was a school principal at Fairlawn Elementary, a school of 350 children. Among her many duties, she was supposed to keep the students, teachers, and staff safe. If the district had given her sixty security measures she was required to follow every day to maintain that safe environment and she had failed to complete thirty of those measures and a gunman had entered her school and killed seventeen students, should she have been entitled to keep her job? Wouldn't the parents have been justified in asking that she be held accountable? Some of

Mostly, all we really wanted was to be listened to.

us were simply asking for that equivalent from the navy. Instead, the commanding officer, Kirk Lippold, was cleared after a brief investigation and offered a stateside promotion, despite failing to follow navy protocols. At the very least, we wanted to know that the president cared about our opinions and cared about us.

I cannot separate this lack of action and lack of engagement surrounding the *USS Cole* with President Bush's reaction to 9/11 and his insistence in going to war in Iraq. Not only was there never any evidence linking Iraq to the terrorist attacks of 9/11, the country has been in utter chaos ever since. ISIS is the direct product of US failures in Iraq. Despite President Clinton clearly demonstrating in his transitional meetings with President Bush that national security analysts viewed the top threats as stemming from Osama bin Laden and Al-Qaeda, and North Korea, President Bush had his sights set on Iraq.[18] To many of the *Cole* family members, it felt as if Bush was able to say that the bombing didn't happen on his watch, so he moved on to his own agenda. And as far as Iraq goes, he'd already made up his mind.

Now that may be an equally important lesson for leaders because no one, no matter that person's overall opinion of George W. Bush, would ever accuse him of wavering. He is definitely the kind of guy who makes his mind up. He commits. Wrong or right, he commits. A more jovial analysis of George W. Bush on this topic is that he was driving down a one-way street in the wrong direction, but he was 100 percent confident about what street he was on. Because he was confident, a whole lot of people jumped on that bus with him. Despite no actual evidence that there were weapons of mass destruction in Iraq, Bush was adamant that the United States needed to invade Iraq and remove Saddam Hussein from power. Joint Resolu-

18   William Jefferson Clinton, *My Life, Bill Clinton* (New York: Knopf, 2004), 754.

tion 114, the Authorization for Use of Military Force against Iraq, passed the Senate by a vote of seventy-seven to twenty-three and the House of Representatives by a vote of 296 to 133.[19] Bush clearly was successful in winning others over by the force of his conviction.

When a leader offers that kind of confidence, people assume that he has expertise or information they don't have access to and there's comfort in following leadership.

> **You don't lead people to tragedy; you lead them to triumph.**

That's why it is so vital that leaders have situational awareness about their decision making, so that they don't lead people down the wrong path. You don't lead people to tragedy; you lead them to triumph.

We must remember that engagement, given or withheld, holds real consequence because people will follow leaders who demonstrate conviction whether or not they should.

---

19   Authorization for Use of Military Force Against Iraq Resolution of 2002, H. J. Res. 114 (107th) Cong. (2002).

CHAPTER 6
MOTIVATE

You can look me in my eyes, see I'm ready for whatever.
Anything don't kill me, make me better.

—T. I., "Motivation"

So many of our everyday actions as leaders are caught up with determining the *who, what, when,* and *where* that factor into our decisions as we guide our organizations forward. These first four elements—the who, what, when, and where—create a blueprint for an action plan. But knowing them doesn't mean that the job will get done. The *why* we need to do it—or why it matters, or why it makes a difference—is what is going to motivate people to action. By providing the *why,* I give my team motivation that leads to action. And in the reverse, if, as a leader, I understand the personal reasons for my team members' desire to be involved, then I can use that *why* to motivate them.

> **Motivation is the fuel for transformation.**

Motivation is the fuel for transformation. We all want to change things. We all want to make things better. Motivation provides the nourishment to keep going, the nourishment to take action, the nourishment to finish. In John Maxwell's *21 Irrefutable Laws of Leadership*, he discusses the "Law of Navigation," reminding us that a leader not only has to know the way but also show the way; you'll get more people to follow you if you show them where you're going.

The goal for every leader should be to help make the organization and the people within it better every day. To accomplish such a goal, and to make certain that those responsible for accomplishing it find meaning and satisfaction in doing so, a leader must be an effective motivator.

> **The goal for every leader should be to help make the organization and the people within it better every day.**

Motivation is something that you have to give, and receive, every day. You can motivate people with words or you can motivate people with actions. I try to do both. I try to lead by example. That kind of leader always has an impact on people. In football, these are the players who show up early all summer long. They are gym rats. They are the perfectionists. When you watch them perform and you are their teammate, you are motivated not to let them down. You want them to succeed so badly that you push yourself to your limits and you execute on every play. You want to help them to succeed because you are motivated by their commitment, by their steadfastness.

You can also motivate with words. You can literally master the power of effective communication and find the right words that convince hearts and minds to take action and finish the job. Effective oral motivation doesn't mean being loud all the time or possessing a big voice like Chuck D's or my dad's. Tony Dungy, the longtime NFL coach, is a great motivator and he never raises his voice. The players who played for Tony Dungy wanted to succeed for him because they always understood his *why*.

We all respond to different motivations. Some athletes did respond to the hard-driving, insult-laden, bruising approach of several of my college coaches, but I certainly never did and that sort of bullying has no place in offices and hospitals. A leader can have high expectations of people without tearing them down. Some people need a good cheerleader in their corner; others need to know the end goal and then be provided greater autonomy for getting there. They all need good examples and they all must know the *why*.

There's a leader at MUSC Health who leads, in part, by making work fun. She's creative in how she motivates. For one motivational tool, she went outside, literally, and gathered several smooth rocks, which she painted and then wrote the words, "You Rock" on them. At the end of the week she went around the department and gave out rocks to the top performers. She took a photo of each of the recipients, put the photos in a PowerPoint presentation, and e-mailed it to the whole team. Those who had led success or stepped beyond expectations were recognized. Those who didn't "rock" that week were motivated to be in her slideshow the next month. What could be a simpler motivating tool than a rock?

I've mentioned my high school history teacher before, Eric Carlson. He didn't speak to high school students as if they were subordinates. He was the kind of teacher who learned alongside his students. On Fridays, he focused on current events, and he would allow the class to decide what they wanted to be taught. By being placed in charge of some of my own learning and offered the opportunity to teach my peers about something that drove my passions, I was motivated to excel. During Black History Month, I was able to teach my class about the Black Panther Party. I recognized that the school curriculum taught us about Martin Luther King but nothing about Malcolm X or Booker T. Washington or W. E. B. Du Bois. I was teaching a class that, largely, didn't look like me and didn't come from the community I came from and at the same time, I was learning things from their unique perspectives on things that interested them.

I've had a number of great motivators in my life like Mr. Carlson. You've met several of them in these pages. Different people we encounter can motivate us in different ways. Among other motivators in my life I have to include people such as my uncle El' Dawn. He is my mom's baby brother and only seven years older than me, so in some ways he is more like a big brother than an uncle. El' Dawn was the first one to share my passion for hip hop. He took me to my first concert. He motivated me to go to college by bringing me onto campus with him when I was a teenager. El' Dawn is a great example of a quiet motivator, one who always listens but doesn't have to say much. Soft-spoken, easy going, quick with a joke, he is simply the sort of person you want to be around. I knew he believed in me, that he was quietly looking out for me, and that was motivational.

I find motivation in other sources too, such as in the words and ideas of the famous motivational speaker Les Brown. I listen to his presentation "Get Your Mind Right" every day.[20] Whether I listen during my ride to work or while I am on the treadmill or, during the summer when the weather is nice and I walk around my neighborhood in the morning, I hear his words at the start of every day.

Another similar force for me entered my life in an unusual way, accidentally meeting an entrepreneur coach at the end of a Bahamas vacation just after I'd been in the ocean praying for God to send

---

20   Les Brown, "Get Your Mind Right," November 20, 2015, https://www.youtube.com/watch?v=M17UTmSDX9A&t=7s.

someone to help me learn to spread the message I felt inside me. Walter Bond is an extremely successful motivational speaker and former NBA player. Every week, Walter provides me with incredible motivation, and he builds accountability around that motivation. If I get frustrated, he brings me back to my purpose. He brings me back to my *why*.

Part of your job, as a leader, is to be that kind of motivator for the people you serve. One part of doing so is to learn from the people who have motivated you. We need to become mentors and coaches, just as we have been the beneficiaries of great mentors in our lives.

PRESIDENTIAL PRINCIPLE NUMBER FOUR

Be a Great Motivator

It is impossible for me to speak about motivation without focusing on my experiences working with President Obama. He was a master motivator. You have already witnessed how the power of his words had me spellbound the very first time I encountered his book, so his ability to motivate me is clear. The best motivators do more than move you to action; they make you want to be a better

> **The best motivators do more than move you to action; they make you want to be a better person.**

person. That is Barack Obama's influence on me. He possesses a number of qualities that I admire greatly and wish to emulate.

If you spend any time with Barack Obama you see how he loves his wife and his daughters unconditionally. He is open in his demonstration of that love and it is obvious that his love is also filled with respect. I want to love my wife the way Barack Obama loves his wife. I want to love my daughter the way Barack Obama loves his daughters and be comfortable with demonstrating that love in any kind of setting. He motivates me to want to be a better husband and a better father.

A second quality we should all wish to possess is his intelligence. No one who has encountered him, or even heard him speak for that matter, would question that Barack Obama is smart. He surrounds himself with smart people, he's well read, he asks questions, and he is a living definition of what it means to be a lifelong learner. That's why I surround myself with people who are smarter than me. I ask questions. I try to understand a little bit about everything. I read a minimum of twenty books a year. The motivation to do so came directly from emulating Barack Obama.

A third quality that motivates me is that Barack Obama is selfless. As I focused on earlier in the book when discussing his desire to serve, he made a selfless decision to serve in public life, to offer himself up as a candidate, as a state legislator, as a US senator, and as a two-term president. That selflessness motivates me to evaluate what I am doing to serve others.

Much of what guided President Obama's desire to serve and reinforced his ability to accomplish change is his ability to see how he can do big things. He doesn't think about the right now, he thinks about the long term. We need leaders with vision. The greatest presidents have been the ones who could see long into the future and lay the groundwork to meet that future. I don't want to see down the street; I want to see around the corner. Barack Obama motivates me to dream big and reach far.

The last quality I wish to focus on regarding Barack Obama is his willingness to be audacious. My first book was titled *The Audacity of Leadership.* I don't think you get anymore audacious than to be a black man in the United States of America with the name of Barack Hussein Obama and not only believe that you can be president of the United States, but you actually run and do it twice. President Obama campaigned on change and hope, for those were values he believed in authentically. He truly wanted positive change directed out of hopefulness for the American people and he set out throughout his presidency to accomplish change that makes people's lives better. That is a root of audacious thinking. I am committed to being the kind of leader and motivator who thinks boldly and who commits with all of my heart.

CHAPTER 7
ACT

You know that it has to be perfectly fitted 'cause I'm committed.
The entertainer and trainer and Kane'll get with it.

—Big Daddy Kane, "Raw"

There's no point in having the tools, the information, and the motivation to do something if you don't take action. The leaders who have the greatest impact on the world are the ones who actually do something. So many of us suffer from paralysis by analysis. We overthink things and obsess over having all of the reports, all of the facts and figures, all of the data points. I'm not discounting the importance of data, but sometimes you can be given so much information that it makes you freeze. You can't get so bogged down in the analysis that you fail to take action.

Action is executing your commitment to do something. I define commitment as doing what you said you would do long after the feeling you had when you said you would do it has left your body. You must be all the way in or all the way out. The greatest leaders don't wade into the water halfway. Barack Obama did not wade into the water halfway when committing to the ACA. George W. Bush did not make half a decision about going to war after 9/11. His father, George H. W. Bush, committed to defending Kuwait and going to war with Saddam Hussein. Impactful leaders act with conviction.

Another example comes from my home state of South Carolina. I served with Nikki Haley in the state legislature prior to her becoming governor. We certainly don't always align on our politics and definitely do not on our vision for health care, but I greatly respect the way she commits to assertive action. Prior to Hurricane Matthew we experienced a storm that featured twenty-one days of rain over the city of Columbia. There was tremendous flood damage. Nikki took immediate executive action to protect life, save property, and lead people

> **Action is executing your commitment to do something. I define commitment as doing what you said you would do long after the feeling you had when you said you would do it has left your body.**

through the crisis. She did the same with Hurricane Matthew. She was decisive about closing interstates and opening shelters and was uncompromising about people's safety. She reacted in a similar way when nine black church members were murdered in an African Methodist Episcopal church in Charleston. The murderer was a racist and Confederate flag sympathizer. After the massacre, Governor Haley called for the removal of the Confederate flag from the statehouse.

To act with conviction means that you must believe in what you are doing. People don't follow leaders who are indecisive. While they expect that you have completed your analysis and believe that you have gathered your facts and have made an informed decision, they want leaders who have chosen a path and committed themselves to action.

Even leaders who act with conviction will make mistakes. In this book I've outlined presidential leadership decisions with which I disagree. Some of those leadership decisions are likely to be labeled as mistakes by historians, such as George W. Bush's decision to invade Iraq on the claim Hussein harbored weapons of mass destruction. But both disagreement and inevitable mistakes are part of the terrain of high level leadership.

Taking action with conviction doesn't preclude you from making a mistake. But when you make a mistake, don't repeat it. Recover from it, evaluate what you did wrong, learn from it, and then take action again. That's the iteration process of leadership. It is essential to quality leadership that you try new methods and attempt thoughtful, creative solutions. Not every experiment will work. John Maxwell says, "Sometimes you win, sometimes you learn." He never uses the word "lose" because failure is not about losing; it's about learning. Improvise, adapt, overcome. If you have the right tools, the right information, and the proper motivation, you will succeed far more often than you fail. Through it all you must continue to act on your *why* with conviction.

Leaders who act with conviction, leaders who desire to have presidential impact in their organizations, are forward thinkers who will inevitably face pushback at times because people naturally resist change. In my career, I have experienced instances when I have been hired into a new organization as a senior leader and faced doubt and challenge from others. I have encountered organizations where some members of a leadership team don't behave as principled leaders should, looking out for the good of their people and their organization. They act instead as if they were feudal lords protecting what they see as their terrain. We've probably all encountered similar circumstances. It's easy, in that kind of environment, to react rather than respond, to become derailed by the negative energy that has emerged because of poor, selfish leadership. In that sort of organization, you have to learn the lesson of leadership and make the commitment to control what you can control, influence what you can influence, and lead where leadership is needed. Rather than react to the naysayers, you must influence others in your organization to whom you have responsibility—your community—by how you serve them, by how you help them solve challenges. I always go back to the popular statement attributed to Gandhi, "Be the change you want to see in the world." These words are not a verbatim quotation of Gandhi's actual words, but they articulate more completely the idea as it applies to leadership:

> **Leaders who desire to have presidential impact in their organizations, are forward thinkers who will inevitably face pushback at times because people naturally resist change.**

If we could change ourselves, the tendencies in the world would also change.

As man changes his own nature, so too does the attitude of the world change towards him ... we need not wait to see what others do.[21]

---

21   Quoted from "General Knowledge about Health: Accidents Snake Bite," chap. 32 of *The Collected Works of Mahatma Gandhi*, vol. 12 (Delhi: Ministry of Information and Broadcasting Publications Division, 1958–1964); originally printed in *Indian Opinion*, September 8, 1913.

What better way to deal with negative people than to be the greatest person that you hope to be? Whoever the role model you have as a leader or whatever best practices you want to implement, start by applying the lessons of that role model, follow the best practices you believe in, be true to the person you are. When you are

> **What better way to deal with negative people than to be the greatest person that you hope to be?**

true to your convictions, when you recognize leadership is rooted in service, when you empower those you serve, positive energy emerges and organizations change in ways that allow them to accomplish their goals.

If you truly wish to lead by empowering those around you, you must become the "master of ceremonies" and follow what I call the "emcee" model of leadership development: E-M-C-E-E (engaging, mentoring, coaching, empowering, elevating). This model starts with engagement, engaging with people at a grass roots level. Then you must mentor people, be their resource and their guide, and provide them a roadmap or blueprint. Next you coach them, you accompany them down that road, you help them when they encounter roadblocks and detours, and you help them improvise, adapt, and overcome so they achieve success. These steps allow you to empower them by providing them the tools to succeed and asking them to assume responsibility and accountability to implement the blueprint, or follow the roadmap. Accomplish all the above and you have people positioned to be elevated. With the application of the emcee approach and the success it generates, you begin to create legacy by providing leadership opportunities, something that will be a primary focus of the next section of the book.

THE **EMCEE** THEORY OF LEADERSHIP DEVELOPMENT

★ ★ ★

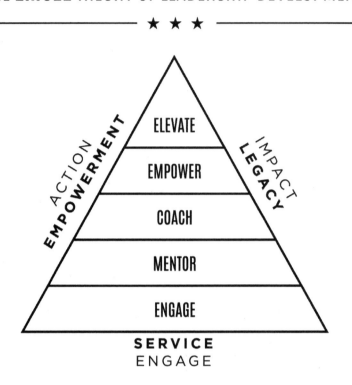

 PRESIDENTIAL PRINCIPLE NUMBER FIVE

Don't Preach What You Don't Know

George Herbert Walker Bush was elected president when I was fifteen. My dad was still in the navy and that meant in 1990, when President Bush formed an international collation to expel Iraqi troops from Kuwait, my father's ship, the *USNS Comfort*, was called up for Desert Storm.

I was seventeen, in high school, and being recruited to play college football. With only five official campus visits to decide where you're going to school, you should not only choose carefully but also bring the most important people in your life with you to help you to make the decision. When I toured NC State with my parents, college was a foreign thing to my dad and he asked a lot of questions. He quickly built a relationship with Robbie Caldwell, the offensive line coach recruiting me, and he loved his weekend on the campus. But immediately on our return home, my dad received notice of his deployment. I was accustomed to my father being called away to serve, but at this moment of making a crucial decision, I wanted dad there with me.

America's clearest memory of war was the failure it had suffered in Vietnam, and President Bush was well aware that the public didn't want a protracted war. He weighed this public sentiment when he asked Congress to declare war against Saddam Hussein and his Iraq regime. Given an environment that was lukewarm about military intervention at best, President Bush made a leadership decision to send Vice President Dan Quayle to three military bases to give speeches in hopes of rallying the American public by speaking to the families of those whose loved ones were deployed to serve. One of those military installations was in Norfolk. As were the other families of the Norfolk Naval Base, we were invited to attend the rally.

We arrived at a hangar filled with 600 people. It was loud, with everyone waving American flags, your typical rally. I wasn't interested. I just wanted my dad home. Now recall that there was a soundtrack of radical hip hop music playing in the back of my head at all times and I had a view consistently reinforced that Bush and Reagan had not been good for the black community. I entered the rally with a biased view about the president, but I still respected him because I knew he had served our country as a US Navy pilot and I held the office of the presidency in high regard.

Almost immediately upon entering the hangar, I was approached by a reporter. Maybe she approached me because I was young, or maybe because, at seventeen, and six feet five inches tall, I tended to stand out. She asked if I was surprised that the president would send the vice president to speak at this event. I didn't understand why she was asking the question and told her so. She said, "Don't you think it's funny that the president would send Dan Quayle, a draft dodger, here? Why would he be asked to speak to military families?" I knew little about politics, so I told her I didn't know what she was talking about. She said Quayle used his connections so he could get into the National Guard and wouldn't have to go to Vietnam. Hearing her, I became angry. I was already unhappy that my dad had been taken away from me and put in danger. To hear that the president had sent a hypocrite to rally the families of military personnel only worsened my mood.

The whole time Vice President Quayle was speaking, I was fuming, for I was thinking how the presidential decision to go to war in Desert Storm had already disrupted our lives and altered my college decisions.

When Quayle finished his speech, I could see he was going to walk the rope line and shake hands with people in the crowd, so I used my size to elbow my way to the front. I wanted to give Dan Quayle a piece of my mind. Quayle worked his way down the line, and when he was in front of me, I reached out to shake his hand so I could get his attention even though I saw he was looking at someone he knew in the crowd, behavior I would one day become accustomed to as I worked among politicians. His disinterest in me only made me angrier, so I squeezed the vice president's hand, yanked his arm, and started to scream at him. Before I could say a coherent sentence, I was grabbed by two US Secret Service agents. They dragged me out of the hangar, through a back lobby, to the parking lot, and they started to handcuff me and put me in a car. My mom arrived, my brothers in tow. She was crying because they didn't know what was happening. The US Secret Service officers looked at my family and then at me, and apparently, they realized I was just a kid and let me go.

Upon reflection on this incident once I was older, what I learned fits into what I call presidential leadership principles. The foremost lesson in my mind remains that, as a leader, you should never send a substitute to deliver difficult news. In my eyes, George Herbert Walker Bush served our country and would have been a much more credible messenger. He would have been delivering a message that he had lived himself. President Bush enlisted in the US Navy immediately after he graduated from Phillips Academy on his eighteenth birthday. He volunteered to serve. Dan Quayle earned his law degree while a member of the National Guard.

> **The foremost lesson in my mind remains that, as a leader, you should never send a substitute to deliver difficult news.**

As I reflect on my own reaction, I believe the second lesson for a leader is to always be wary of the media, especially those who go looking for salacious stories, and make certain you know your facts and you are informed about the context of those areas for which you are responsible. Be a good enough critical thinker to recognize the difference between honest reporters searching for facts and those looking to sell their story or inflame those they interview.

The third lesson I take away from the experience is also one I apply to myself: always remain in control of your emotions. In this instance, because I let my emotions get the best of me, they nearly put me in a situation from which I might never have recovered.

The final lesson I take away from this presidential encounter was delivered by that moment with Dan Quayle: never, ever preach what you don't practice.

Be authentic. Be true to who you are. Leaders must act with conviction.

Be authentic. Be true to who you are. Leaders must act with conviction. You can't act on convictions you don't hold.

PART III

LEGACY

Success without a successor is a failure.

—Myles Munroe

CHAPTER 8
WHAT I'M HERE FOR

And while some choose greed, I choose to plant seeds.

—*Gang Starr,* "What I'm Here 4"

After Cherone's death, I turned, in part, to where I always turn—hip hop—to grieve and to heal. Mostly, I put in the work to help others who needed help, as I felt serving others was the best way I could remember Cherone and create a legacy that would honor him. In 1999, prior to starting graduate school and prior to Cherone's death, Lenora Bush Reese had asked me to serve on the board of directors for South Carolina Fair Share. In a matter of years, I had gone from being a staff member as my first "real" job to serving on the board. I was deeply honored. I tried to be a voice for the families of the *Cole* victims as well. In those years I thought often about these lines from Gang Starr's song, "Robbin Hood Theory":

> *If I wasn't kickin' rhymes I'd be kickin' down doors*
> *Creatin' social change and defendin' the poor.*

With Cherone's death, parts of my life felt as if they were shutting down, while others—my marriage with Tiffany, my work in school, this opportunity to serve Fair Share—made me feel like my life was opening up, and those opposing feelings made me want to work harder.

During my time on the board, Lenora announced her decision to leave Fair Share. After considering a number of applicants and not finding one that satisfied the executive search committee, the chair of the board, Joanne Emerson, met with John Ruoff, unbeknownst to me. John had been the executive director, after founding Fair Share in 1986, until he stepped down in 1995, supporting Lenora as his replacement because he believed the organization needed to be led by a woman of color. John had stayed on as a staff member, doing legislative policy work. A brilliant man, he was deeply respected and had been an important mentor to me, teaching me a great deal about South Carolina politics and the legislative process. John told Joanne that I should be the next executive director. I had never considered applying for the position because I didn't think I was worthy to replace Lenora.

I was flabbergasted and flattered when they invited me to interview. And when they offered me the position, they held it for me for three months until I graduated with my master's degree. Becoming executive director of South Carolina Fair Share was one of the most empowering experiences of my professional career. I believed in the work and the mission and the value of the organization.

Lenora gave me great advice that I continue to share when it comes to running a nonprofit. She said, "Anton, you can be a good executive director, you can be a good development director, or a good program director, but you can't be all three. You have to choose." My staff provided me with support so that I could concentrate on the executive director role and developing the vision for the organization's future. I believed we could change poor people's experiences in South Carolina if we focused on grassroots outreach and developed leadership around the state. I believed reaching people in the streets was how we would get politicians to be responsive. We stole a page from a famous South Carolina white supremacist and former governor, Pitchfork Ben Tillman, who had systematically disenfranchised the black majority during Reconstruction by acting on his belief that "South Carolina is small enough that if you can have one leader in every county, you can control what happens in the state." We took that philosophy, turned it on its head, and set about developing progressive community leaders in every county. We built a grassroots movement of people-power leaders who would inspire and create change in their home communities on issues they cared about.

Becoming executive director of South Carolina Fair Share was one of the most empowering experiences of my professional career. I believed in the work and the mission and the value of the organization.

Despite success at Fair Share, I continued to struggle to understand Cherone's death. One person who was helpful to me was the talented pastor of the church Tiffany and I attended, Barry Mitchell. Barry could see my pain and told me, "Anton, I can't give you answers why your brother was killed. But I can tell you that the answers are there in the Bible." I began to study the Bible closely and found comfort and guidance there, and on February 10, 2002, I was saved and born again.

My faith helped me continue the work of serving "the least of these," and in 2003 I was approached by Charlene Sinclair, from the Center for Community Change, with another opportunity. She asked, "What do you think about building something that would put poor people's issues on the front page, nationally? And what if we did it in South Carolina? If we can get all of the presidential candidates and George Bush in the room together, wouldn't that be powerful?" What emerged from our conversation was the formation of a powerful grassroots coalition. A partnership formed between CCC and Fair Share and approached every social justice organization in the state—veteran's groups, the NAACP, fair housing activists, and health care organizations, among others—and brought their different interests together through the commonality that they all served underrepresented people without voice in the political process. We helped them focus on issues that were not being addressed by any candidate, least of all, the current president. We built a people's agenda focused on economic justice.

From there, we nationalized and brought in busloads of activists to march in Columbia. In the end, there were sixty organizations from thirty-five states represented and all the 2004 Democratic presidential candidates attended. The events were covered nationally. At the end of a day filled with activities and forums, we had 3,000 people in a Columbia auditorium asking questions of candidates about what they would do to improve the plight for poor people in America. And the next day we sent all those activists out to knock on doors to register voters and share news of the people's agenda.

The candidates included Wesley Clark. Stacey Brayboy worked on his campaign. Stacey and I had met previously at a training event in Detroit called Democratic Gain. While she was in South Carolina, Stacey and I were having coffee together when she told me, "Anton, you are a sleeper." I had no idea what she meant. She said, "You're going to be a great candidate and a great elected official, but nobody is gonna see you coming. They don't know about you because you don't do political work. If you jumped into politics, you're gonna come out of nowhere and surprise people." And then, after the success of the people's agenda, Charlene Sinclair said to me, "Okay, so when are we running you for governor? Because you did a phenomenal job at organizing the People's Agenda."

I had never seen myself as a political candidate, despite people having suggested otherwise. That Detroit training had taught me how to use data analysis and how to win a campaign. Charlene's and Stacey's belief in me sparked something. Over the next couple of years, I continued to think about what they had said, and I started to learn the political landscape. After Tiffany became pregnant in 2004, we moved to the suburbs. Part of me had been against the move because I didn't think a progressive candidate could win there. There we were, living in the suburbs near where Tiffany had grown up, and we had a new baby, Ashley, and every night we couldn't get her to sleep because there were cars driving by with booming stereo systems. I thought, "That's a lot of hip hop being played in the suburbs."

Urban sprawl, combined with upward mobility, was transforming my legislative district. Developers were buying tracks of land and building houses, while the city tore down public housing and gave low income residents Section 8 vouchers, whose recipients wanted their kids to go to the better schools in the suburbs. Middle class black families began to relocate from the urban center. I started riding through suburban neighborhoods, looking for historically black college fraternity and sorority car tags and discovering more and more black families. I thought that if they knew who I was and what I had done, there might be a chance I could build a political base. My legislative district had become 32 percent African American. I knew I couldn't win with that percentage, but if I could campaign to moderate white voters, I could win with 20 percent of their vote.

In 2006 I took my long-shot attempt at the state legislative seat against a twelve-year incumbent Republican. I came within 298 votes of winning in a Republican-dominated district that had never elected an African American.

In the two years between that loss and my decision to run again, I had some monumental personal growth experiences. Just weeks after losing the election in 2006, I read Barack Obama's book while I was at the Washington, D.C. airport. The words on the page inspired me to get involved in his long-shot presidential campaign. At the time, it was impossible for most people to get close to Barack Obama, the most talked about "potential" presidential candidate in late 2006. I was inspired that he had the audacity to believe he could be president. Knowing I could learn from him, I vowed that I would do what I could to see that he won the South Carolina presidential primary and I made good on that commitment. Even though I was a political novice—I had run for office one time and lost and had no national political connections—I got myself into Barack Obama's presidential campaign the only way I knew how: I called him. When most people call someone, they may try two or three times, and if they don't get a return phone call, they quit and move on. I didn't quit. I didn't move on. I called his Senate office in D.C. multiple times. I sent multiple e-mails. I called his office in Chicago repeatedly. Finally, when I called his office

> **I came within 298 votes of winning in a Republican-dominated district that had never elected an African American.**

in southern Illinois, I managed, somehow, to get a message through. Barack Obama personally called me back.

It was a brief phone call, but I told Senator Obama, "I don't know politics, but I do know South Carolina. You need somebody on your team who understands the state." My phone rang two minutes after we hung up and it was his deputy campaign manager, Steve Hildebrand. We arranged a meeting for a week later when I was going to be in D.C. for the Families USA conference, where I was being named Consumer Health Advocate of the Year. Barack Obama was scheduled as a keynote speaker.

I met Steve Hildebrand in the Mayflower Hotel lobby, as planned. At the end of our discussion, I asked if I could meet with Obama while he was at the conference. He said it was unlikely, because the senator had an impossible schedule as he was preparing to give a Democratic response to the State of the Union address.

That night I went to dinner with some friends, Ayo and Gil Winters. Gil was a former football player at Duke. When I shared my story of how I got Barack Obama to return my phone call, Gil told me about a former Duke football player named Reggie Love who worked for Senator Obama as his Senate aide. He said that he and Reggie were friends and that it might be helpful to connect with Reggie.

The next day, as the conference started, I ran into Regina Wise, who was on the conference planning committee. We were talking when she excused herself to meet someone, and I watched her approach a tall, dark, skinny guy. I knew Regina handled logistics and watching her talk to a guy who matched Gil's description, I surmised he had to be Reggie Love.

I made a beeline to Reggie, introduced myself and shared my connections to Gil and Steve Hildebrand. I added that I had talked to Senator Obama the week before. I said, "They're talking about bringing me on the campaign, so I figured it'd be good for me to meet the candidate." Reggie replied that he didn't know if he could make it happen, but he accepted the business card I gave him.

The next day, when Obama was scheduled to speak, I was asked to sit in the balcony along with the other conference VIPs. Barack Obama entered the auditorium and took a seat on the stage. I saw him pull out his Blackberry and type something. Then, I got an e-mail message on my Blackberry from Reggie Love asking if I could meet Obama at stage door when his speech ended. He told me I'd have to be there waiting or I would miss him. Gratefully, the staircase bottomed out right by the stage door. I called out, "Senator Obama, I'm Anton Gunn." Two security personnel blocked me from reaching him. He heard me and said, "Oh, hello! Let him through." I grabbed Tiffany's hand and we were escorted into the Mayflower's kitchen. Obama shook my hand, and I introduced Tiffany. He said hello to her and asked, "Ma'am, would you mind if I borrowed your husband for a few minutes?" Then he turned to me and asked, "Do you mind taking a ride with me?" We walked out of the side door to a two-door Saab hatchback. Obama opened the passenger door and said, "I guess you've got to get in the back." I squeezed my six feet five inches and 300 pounds into the back seat of a two-door Saab. The driver handed the senator a turkey sandwich and apple juice. Obama turned to me and said, "You see how they do me?"

For that twenty-minute ride from the Mayflower Hotel to the Senate office building, we talked about life, about family, about our daughters, and our mothers-in-law. And then we talked about the campaign. He told me that the demands of Iowa wouldn't allow him much time in South Carolina, so he needed people who could be his eyes and ears. The only thing I wanted to be for Barack Obama was a surrogate. I would happily use my skills as an inspirational speaker and travel around South Carolina telling people why Barack Obama should be president. I just wanted to be on his team, to be in his presence.

He said, "You played college football?" I told him I did. "What position?"

"Offensive line."

He said, "That's good. You're used to getting beat up."

"Yeah," I said, "but I dish out as much punishment as I get."

"Good. I need some tough people because it's going to be a tough campaign. I need someone who can be strong for me in South Carolina."

I told him he'd found the right man. Then he asked me, "Is there anything you need to say to me?"

I said, "I've got two things to tell you. Number one, when I'm with you, I'm loyal to the end. Number two, I'm always going to be transparent with you, which means when you start fucking up, I'm going to tell you you're fucking up." And I said, "I need you to be okay with that."

"Oh, I'm okay with that."

We reached his office and immediately a staffer ran up and said he had to be in the Foreign Relations Committee meeting. Obama turned to me and shook my hand. "The door is out that way to the left. You should be able to get a cab." I stepped out into the January cold. I had no hat and no jacket. I wasn't sure I had a wallet to pay the cab fare. That was on the 26th, and on the same day a year later, Obama won the South Carolina primary. A week after our meeting, Steve Hildebrand called and offered me a job as a state director for the Obama Campaign.

I was thirty-four years old and a political novice. I called Stacey Brayboy and told her what had happened. She, unlike me, had worked for multiple Democratic political campaigns. She told me, "Anton, the whole world is trying to get close to Barack Obama, and nobody can, and you're riding around in the car with him. How the hell did you pull that off?" She encouraged me to take the job and offered to coach me by phone in the evenings. Ultimately, knowing how much I needed to learn, I rejected the position of state campaign director and instead, accepted the job of political director, and after talking to Stacey for weeks, I convinced her to apply. Then I called Steve Hildebrand and told him that we would lose if we didn't have an African American woman as our state campaign director.

My interest in working on Obama's campaign was to be up close and personal with the candidate running for president, to learn from him, and additionally, to apply that learning to a second run to serve in the legislature. The whole year working on Obama's campaign was filled with incredible challenges and opportunities. I grew as a person, became more sophisticated as a politician, and most importantly, I garnered Tiffany's support, which gave me the confidence to run again and win. The first time around, she'd been reluctant because she doesn't enjoy being in the spotlight. The game changer for Tiffany was a conversation she had with Michelle Obama during the 2008 primary. Michele accompanied us to church during a campaign visit and told Tiffany about her own reluctance with her husband's involvement in politics but explained that she knew he was bright and gifted and had value to add to people's lives. "Who am I," she asked Tiffany, "to rob the community of what he adds because I want him just to be my husband?"

For my second campaign, I perfected the Obama organizing model, from community organization of house meetings to grassroots fundraising from individual, diverse donors. I got more people involved, and I learned not to ignore any constituency. I took a leave of absence from Fair Share and went all-in on the campaign.

Tiffany, appreciative what Michelle Obama had shared with her, was supportive of me, even if she wasn't the happiest camper when left alone with a three-and-a-half year-old and balancing work as a real estate agent while I was working sixteen hours a day campaigning. I put 33,000 miles on my car, went through a set of tires, and had thirteen oil changes in twelve months. My hard work and stronger organizing paid off. On November 4, 2008, I was elected to the South Carolina House of Representatives, becoming the first African American in history to represent my district.

On November 4, 2008, I was elected to the South Carolina House of Representatives, becoming the first African American in history to represent my district.

What I enjoyed once I took my seat in the legislature was the constituent service, as well as the ready media access that could benefit causes I represented on behalf of my constituents. But I hated the internal politics, which were omnipresent. I was introduced to a system where Republicans were forced to go to their corner and put on their red jersey with an R on the front and I was supposed to go to my corner and put on my blue D jersey.

In my second session, I proposed a common sense budget amendment that called for transparency, essentially asking that the various fees citizens paid to the state be traced rather than simply be moved blindly to the general fund. I succeeded in getting the majority of the chamber to vote for it. But there was an ultra-Republican from Myrtle Beach named Thad Viers, who became angry because his colleagues had voted for an idea that came from a "liberal Democrat from Richland County" and he tried to block its passage. That was the political reality I found. Yet even a guy such as Viers could be different outside politics. I recall one occasion when we both arrived late for an event at the governor's mansion, so we ended up sitting in the back of the room together, near the kitchen entrance. Governor Sanford had served fried chicken. Thad turned to me at one point and said, smiling, "Man, if my constituents saw me right now, they'd run me out of office. I can't be caught sitting by the kitchen with the black Obama radical with a liberal socialist agenda." I replied to his joke, saying, "Well, I'm losing my street credibility sitting beside you, knowing that you are a right-wing, Tea Party, hate-everything-I-like Republican." That was the beginning of a friendship between us outside the chamber, but when it came time to vote, he could never agree with anything I stood for. I could never understand the cognitive dissonance of having good ideas and building good relationships, yet

> I could never understand the cognitive dissonance of having good ideas and building good relationships, yet seeing those ideas squashed and relationships squandered because of partisanship or the fear of how you might look in the eyes of party leaders and constituents.

seeing those ideas squashed and relationships squandered because of partisanship or the fear of how you might look in the eyes of party leaders and constituents.

My time in the legislature was further frustrated by a difficult choice I had to make: either give up my seat or resign my position at Fair Share. There were state ethics laws that prohibited any organization affiliated with a member of the general assembly from lobbying the general assembly. Rather than see Fair Share unable to develop a legislative agenda that could benefit the people it represented, I stepped aside. Sometimes leadership requires making personal sacrifice, and I made a significant sacrifice in order to serve the people of South Carolina by giving up my livelihood with Fair Share and doing so in the middle of the 2008 economic recession that had hit my family hard.

One factor in the economic hardship we faced along with so many other Americans was the $17,000 in medical debt we had accrued because Blue Cross and Blue Shield denied coverage for Tiffany's pregnancy. Like millions, I was denied coverage for simply not checking a box on the application form—the ACA made sure a simple mistake like this wouldn't prevent others from having insurance coverage.

In those lean financial years after my election in 2008, I benefited from lots of examples of how investing in people can create returns. Jeremy Bird, who had been the field director when we worked together on Obama's campaign, reached out to me for help from his new position with the Democratic National Committee. They were looking for someone to develop Democratic grassroots leadership through a group called Organizing for America. Jeremy brought me in as a consultant, and between that and what was then my fledgling work as a leadership speaker, I was able to supplement my legislator salary and continue to try and do good work for people.

It was another example of investment that ultimately led me to a position with Health and Human Services (HHS). When I was the political director with the Obama campaign, on the advice of my college fraternity brother Steve Benjamin, I interviewed and hired Mike McCauley as a deputy to focus on reaching white Democrats. We jokingly referred to Mike's work on the campaign as the "8 Mile Outreach." This referenced Mike's initials "M and M" and Eminem, the white rap star, whose real name was Marshall Mathers and whose semi-autobiographical movie *8 Mile* referenced 8 Mile Road, the highway between the predominantly black city of Detroit and the predominantly white Oakland and Macom County suburbs. I hired Mike in part to do political outreach across racial lines in the Democratic Primary. Mike did tremendous work for the Obama campaign. After the inauguration, Mike accepted a job at HHS as the White House liaison, tasked with filling the departmental presidential appointments. In March 2010, Mike reached out for help finding suitable candidates. He told me, "Anton, we've appointed five regional directors, and I'm calling you because we need to find somebody for the southeast. We need somebody who, first of all, knows health care, but really, we need somebody who knows how to navigate southern politics because this region is the most hostile to Barack Obama." Mike, despite working with me in advance of the South Carolina primary, didn't know me well or know of the career I had established as a health care policy advocate. I told him, "Mike, the person you are describing is me." I was appointed as the regional director of HHS Region IV on August 12, 2010. When I accepted appointment in the Obama administration, the clerk of the house told me I did not need to immediately resign from the South

Carolina House of Representatives as the legislative season didn't begin until January. My replacement would be sworn in before the next legislative season, so I announced that I would not be seeking reelection to the South Carolina House of Representatives. It was a great honor to serve the people of South Carolina. I viewed it as a greater honor to serve the president of the United States, something I saw as an extension of what my brother and my dad had done.

I arrived in Atlanta and got immediately to work. The ACA had already become law and people had started trying to dissect what was in it. Some were honestly trying to learn, but others were more interested in using provisions of the law to confuse, distract, dispute, and divide. I traveled extensively to talk to groups about what was in the ACA and the benefits of the law. We faced members of Congress who would tell bold-faced lies about what the law included. We were in a constant battle of trying to educate people while they were hearing the complete opposite message from their governors, members of Congress, and media pundits. The amount of lies and misinformation was overwhelming. People would say things like, "If you signed up for Obamacare, they're going to implant you with a chip so they can track where you go."

I was on an airplane three to four days a week, every week, for nineteen months. I had eight states under my purview. I did radio and television interviews and Town Hall meetings for state legislators and congressmen. I attended kick-off events and ribbon cuttings for community health centers. I seized every opportunity to educate Americans. Every venue was a different experience depending on the preconception peopled entered with, but by providing the facts, people began to sit forward in their seats. I did 160 speeches in a year. I saw momentum in the individual rooms where I spoke, but even though I could reach twenty-five or fifty or three hundred people at a time, with sixty-three million people in an eight-state region. I wasn't putting a dent in the overall narrative. Meanwhile, I was responsible for all the other areas of HHS oversight in the region, beyond the ACA, which included speaking at training sessions for Medicare enrollees, advocating on behalf of the Administration on Aging, and meeting with Native American tribal leaders on medical support and services. I was exhausted. It quickly became pointless to move my family to Atlanta since I was never there, so I commuted to Columbia every weekend, getting up at 3:00 a.m. every Sunday to start the drive back to work.

The job was exhausting and exhilarating at the same time and taught me a great deal about leadership. The way HHS is structured, the director is the only political appointee in a region filled with career employees. As a political appointee, I didn't have authority to hire and fire. Technically, the employees didn't report to me, but as the regional leader, I needed to make sure they were helping me carry out the secretary's and the president's priorities. I understood I could not be a coercive leader. If I wanted cooperation and good outcomes, I had to use the leadership principles that I've laid out in this book. I had to serve them, and so, if any regional employee wanted me to come and speak at an event, I showed up. If I could help solve a problem, I did so. I supported and empowered them to execute their priorities. I lived the principles I teach. When I was promoted to D.C. in 2012 to become the director of the External Affairs division, several federal employees approached me and said

The job was exhausting and exhilarating at the same time and taught me a great deal about leadership.

that they were more motivated about their job than they had ever been in their career.

When I got to D.C., I found the HHS main office was completely different from the regional office. Everyone who works in the immediate office of the HHS secretary is a political appointee. I learned quickly that there were many internal politics. Many battled for face time with Secretary Sebelius. And there were factions within the department: those who arrived because of affiliations with Tom Daschle, who was originally supposed to be the HHS nominee; those loyal to Ted Kennedy because of his work in health care; and those who had worked on health care policy with Hillary Clinton. I had a great team, but trying to move ideas among the factions was difficult. Some of the people senior to me at HHS and in the White House had no idea what was in the ACA and they were so afraid of being attacked by the Republican Congress that they failed to take action. Every presentation I gave was subject to editing by the White House Healthcare Communications Team. The White House staffers were skilled campaigners but lacked government experience. Some thought they were better messengers than Secretary Sebelius, a two-term governor and former state insurance commissioner. They went so far as to keep her from doing Sunday morning national television interviews. As if we didn't already face an uphill battle against those who were smearing the facts about the ACA, we were behind in all aspects of the roll-out because of in-fighting, ineptitude, and an insistence that we wait until after the November elections. Often it felt that individuals were engaged in internal sabotage. There were many sad lessons about failures of leadership including lack of action, lack of engagement, lack of empowerment.

All the while, we were tasked with getting seven million people to enroll for health care, particularly those under the age of thirty-five. We were creative in our outreach despite the obstacles and found innovative ways to reach young people through enlisting the help of celebrities, musicians, and comedians. We succeeded in getting LL Cool J and Katy Perry involved. We were in a difficult position because we had people telling blatant lies about the ACA and yet we could not call them out as liars. Instead, we were limited to presenting the facts. As an HHS spokesperson, I was constantly speaking in venues where the audience members were African Americans, and it became more and more apparent to me that what we had thought were the best means of reaching young black people were not politically expedient. A lot of popular figures younger people paid the most attention to had questionable backgrounds or used a lot of foul language. They were not the sort of people we could invite to the White House. Yet, if young people did not sign up for health care, our mission was in jeopardy. I made a decision based on how I could accomplish the greatest good. I approached Valerie Jarrett and Michael Strautmanis and I told them that I would never be able to involve popular music artists such as Wiz Khalifa and Rick Ross to help us as long as I was a government employee. I

There were many sad lessons about failures of leadership including lack of action, lack of engagement, lack of empowerment.

proposed that I leave my position and go out on my own to travel and speak on behalf of the ACA. And that's what I did for the next three months. On April 1, 2014, the numbers came in and we succeeded in enrolling seven million people.

I spent that summer actively growing my business as a consultant, health care entrepreneur, and professional speaker and was named a fall 2014 Resident Fellow at the Harvard Institute of Politics. There I led a study group for a course titled "Amazed and Confused, the Politics and the Process of Implementing Healthcare Reform." After my time at Harvard, I accepted the positions I currently hold as executive director of Community Health Innovation and chief diversity officer at MUSC.

At MUSC, and within my continuous engagement as a leadership coach, I act on and share the leadership principles explored in this book. I live my values, as all leaders must. They are not mere words but lessons I have observed in working alongside impactful leaders, and lessons I have learned through a career of leadership service.

On April 1, 2014, the numbers came in and we succeeded in enrolling seven million people.

CHAPTER 9
GROW THROUGH ADVERSITY

Even when the condition is critical, when the livin
is miserable, your position is pivotal ...

—Talib Kweli, "Get By"

Nobody lives a life free from adversity. You know that at some point in time your number is going to come up. Whether my number came up when I had an eighty-seven mind-set and was in a fifty-nine situation, when my brother was killed, or when I faced battles with entrenched opponents of health care reform, I have faced adversity. I don't think the adversity I have encountered is more significant than anyone else's, but I think about my past struggles and experiences in a way that allows me to process them for better future performance and improvement. What we must realize is that when things go wrong, you can't go wrong with them. You've must have a mind-set of mental preparation for the inevitability that you will face adversity.

Leadership development is always about *growing* through adversity, not just going through it. Adversity is not something you simply overcome; you must learn from it. Growth is about seizing the opportunity to process and reflect on what you're going to do differently the next time. You learn to create an internal environment of resiliency and strength. You do that by knowing that difficult times are going to come and knowing they won't be permanent. A lot of us repeat the same mistakes, not because we're dumb or we're hardheaded. Rather, we never processed the mistake the first time. We never took stock of what went right and what went wrong.

When I think about applying these principles of growth, I can't help but think of Hank Campbell, who played football with me at the University South Carolina. Hank wasn't on a scholarship, so he already had an uphill battle on a SEC football team. Hank was a good player, and like other walk-on players who showed talent and tenacity, he was a contributor. But Hank spent too much time during his first couple of years playing Tecmo Bowl. He didn't go to class and failed school. My experience with others like him was that we never saw them again. Either they never could get it together to return or they were too embarrassed. That wasn't Hank. Hank came back. He had lost his jersey number in the intervening year, but he returned and performed at the highest level. He worked so hard and so faithfully that he earned his spot as our starting middle linebacker and became the leader of the defense. He became the kind of player who gave me a headache and a concussion at almost every practice. He single-handedly made a play against fifteenth-ranked Tennessee that kept them from scoring a two-point conversion and won us the game. Hank didn't let adversity dictate how he was going

> **Leadership development is always about growing through adversity, not just going through it.**

to perform. I watched him overcome whatever was put in front of him. He was an impact player.

My parents take Hank's example to an entirely new level. Losing a child is the most devastating thing that can happen to a parent. You're not supposed to outlive your children. When Cherone was killed, it would have been entirely understandable if they had given up on the world. No one would have blamed them if they had decided to pour their lives into the family we had left. Instead, my parents took on a life of service in my brother's memory. Instead of leaning out, they leaned in. They chose to serve US Veterans in need. I have tried to live my life by their example.

Overcoming adversity is about filling yourself with positivity when you feel negative. My parents were in pain. Instead of letting that pain dictate how they lived their lives, they set an affirmative strategy to get involved in something bigger than themselves that would add value to others and, at the same time, add value to themselves.

We have to do something parallel to their example as leaders. When our organizations face hard times, we have to lean in, problem-solve, and find positive outcomes. We learn from the mistakes we make and then we create a learning environment rather than a punitive one.

Health care provides a good model by applying root cause analysis, and we should embrace it fully. In cases where a patient dies or something goes wrong that causes a patient harm, health care leaders make an objective analysis to determine what its root cause was. This should be our response with all mistakes: assess what happened and why. Did we know what the right things to do were? Did we do them? If we didn't, why not?

Once a root cause is determined, leaders take corrective measures for the future. It's a coaching and counseling model. Mistakes happen. Human error is natural. If we only punish the individual who made the mistake, nobody gets better from it. The only time our response should be punitive is when we determine the person *knowingly* did the wrong thing. There are people who know what the right thing to do is, but they engage in risky behavior. They cut corners. They do things unnecessarily. Workaround is a bad word. If you need to do a workaround, that means your process is broken, inefficient, ineffective. Instead of workarounds, we need to fix the problem. A mind-set focused on fixing problems creates a safety culture. A proper safety culture is a learning culture, one that says we are going to learn from every mistake.

With a learning culture in place, we need to create a reporting culture. If you do something wrong, I'm going to tell somebody you did something wrong. And I'm going to tell *you* that you did something wrong. Now, I'm not trying to get you in trouble, I'm simply reporting your mistake because I've observed the mistake and it's important for us to not make mistakes. We create a culture where everybody understands that we report and learn together for the safety of others. This approach in health care is known as a Just Culture.[22]

The military has a process that is nearly parallel in the form of After Action Reports.[23] These models from the military and health care can apply in every industry. Their commonality is that they form

---

22   Philip G. Boysen, "Just Culture: A Foundation for Balanced Accountability and Patient Safety," *The Ochsner Journal* 13, no. 3 (Fall 2013): 400–406; https://www.ncbi.nlm.nih.gov/pmc/articles/PMC3776518/.

23   "A Leader's Guide to After-Action Reviews," Department of the Army, September 1993, http://www.au.af.mil/au/awc/awcgate/army/tc_25-20/tc25-20.pdf.

intentional processes with cultures that operate from a desire for the opportunity to grow through adversity.

If we are going to learn from our mistakes, we cannot become victims of analysis-paralysis. There are some companies, particularly sales companies, that love to hire former college and professional athletes because they know how to analyze and not dwell. They understand they are not going to win every game in their career. Athletes know that if you lose a game on Saturday, you've got twenty-four hours to analyze what went wrong and figure out what you need to do better. But you must then forget about the last game and focus on the next one. The following Saturday provides you another opportunity to be successful. As leaders we can learn from athletes because we tend to agonize over our losses much more than we analyze victories. And so, you learn more from the loss. I take such lessons to heart and have created a mind-set that believes I'm going to win overall. At the end of the day, I'm going to win. But I'm going to win because I've learned so much from the losses that I'm going to fail forward and I'm going to fail fast.

It's important to remember that adversity introduces leaders to themselves. The real personality always comes out when times are hard. This is why you want to be reflective as you're going through adversity. Losing my brother in a terrorist attack showed me so

Losing my brother in a terrorist attack showed me so much about who I am as a person and who I was going to be for others.

much about who I am as a person and who I was going to be for others. That adversity helped me become the leader I wanted to see in the world.

As are individuals, organizations are also tested in times of adversity. Every organization has a mission. But the question organizations must ask is whether they are embodying their mission in their work and in their employees' lives. Then they have to assess the fulfillment of the mission within the smaller units that make up the organization and the people who make up those units. They must assess if those people are living their values.

Finally—and this is as true for organizations as it is for individual leaders—if you want to achieve your mission and be capable of growing through adversity, you have to find the greatest among you and replicate their leadership. You must model good leaders who execute good leadership practices. Most rational people would list Kobe Bryant as one of the top five best NBA players ever. He had an excellent game and won five NBA Championships. I would argue that Kobe Bryant modeled his game after Michael Jordan. The same way Kobe modeled basketball excellence, I openly model much of my leadership by closely observing Barack Obama.

Leaders need to find those who have come before them and study them closely. Learn from them. Replicate the best of what they represent. And then be the leader you want to see.

PRESIDENTIAL PRINCIPLE NUMBER SIX

Accept Accountability and Share Responsibility

I have encountered no better role model for how one can grow through adversity than Barack Obama. He faced eight years battling many who wished to delegitimize his leadership and those who could not accept a black man as their president. Yet he consistently embraced the adversity he faced with strength, grace, and humor. He never flinched. He never blamed others. He never stopped providing leadership and vision, hope and empowerment. In my years working within his administration and even earlier, meeting him for the first time in that Mayflower Hotel kitchen, I watched how he handled the adversity he met. I watched and I learned.

Perhaps I'd been guilty of labeling him myself before I knew the man Barack Obama is, for I have shared my first reaction to rumors he was planning a presidential run back when I first heard his name: "No one in America is going to vote for a black man named Barack Hussein Obama." He proved me wrong. He overcame centuries of racism, overcame a name some on the far right wished to brand with links to those they associated with terrorism. He encountered the constant barrage of negativity and was called everything but a child of God by Tea Party supporters and ultraconservatives, and yet he never let it bother him.

He stared down the challenges to the ACA, his number-one domestic accomplishment and the centerpiece of his legacy, both those from opponents who battled him before its passage and throughout the years after, and from those responsible for its implementation. In the years from its passage in 2010 until he left office in 2017, the House of Representatives has considered eighty-three resolutions to repeal, deauthorize, defund, or otherwise destroy his signature legislation, and yet, rather than engaging them with bitterness or defensiveness, President Obama consistently spoke about the ACA's successes, that nearly twenty million Americans gained health insurance after its passage, that no longer can people be denied coverage due to pre-existing conditions, that families will no longer have to go into debt because of paperwork errors, as Tiffany and I endured. No one will forget when the ACA enrollment website crashed on its first day. At any moment in time, he could have fired everyone connected to its development for incompetence and gross negligence and started all over, but he didn't focus on what went wrong; he focused on how we were going to clean it up and get it right. Never once did he show anyone publicly that he was not in control. As great leaders must, he remained forward focused and solution oriented. He analyzed the mistake to know what went wrong but did not continue to dwell on it.

I had seen his ability to remain calm in the face of adversity from early on in the 2008 primary campaign. We had organized a free gospel concert in Columbia as an outreach event to draw African American church-going voters. The concert featured four nationally recognized recording artists and included Donnie McClurkin, who said that he believed prayer had delivered him from homosexuality.[24] Needless to say, the LGBT community was enraged. McClurkin's personal beliefs nearly blew up the entire campaign and risked creating division between the LGBT and African American communities, and yet you never once saw Obama get frustrated with either side. Instead, he showed both groups a vision that demonstrated that he did not share McClurkin's beliefs and that he was consistent in taking action on Christian principles of unconditional love and acceptance.

It was a similar approach to what I later saw him take with the ACA website fiasco. I was convinced that much of the problem leading up to the website crash originated in a combination of incompetence among some bureaucrats and internal sabotage among partisans within HHS and the White House. I vividly recall a phone confer-

---

24   "Obama Supporter: 'God Delivered Me from Homosexuality,'" CNN Politics, October 29, 2007, http://politicalticker.blogs.cnn.com/2007/10/29/ obama-supporter-god-delivered-me-from-homosexuality/.

ence, in the midst of that period, where I was yelled at by someone who refused to accept responsibility for failures within the website roll-out and had tried instead to cast blame onto the outreach work my team and I had done. Hearing such false accusations, I really wanted to see Obama fire those responsible for the website failure. And in this meeting, I badly wanted to tell the person yelling at me exactly what I thought. But I followed President Obama's lead. Rather than react, I responded. I made a very clear statement about what I hoped could be done to correct the situation and reminded everyone that our mission needed to focus on getting people enrolled. That's the course Obama had taken. He got to work fixing the problem. In the end I realized that, maybe, he had the right foresight to not overreact and fire people, which would have demoralized everyone else. Instead, he said, "Hey, we messed up; let's get it right."

That's the kind of approach that Barack Obama takes to everything. We acknowledged our failure but we still achieved our goal. He had inherited so many other difficulties as he entered his presidency that he was well equipped to manage this one. In President Barack Obama's first term, our economy was in free fall, losing 700,000 jobs a month. He reacted with bold moves to right the economy and create jobs just as he addressed the lending habits that helped create the housing crisis. Several of his cabinet members were frustrated that they weren't being used for their expertise. They were accomplishing great things in their departments, but when it came to the national narrative on what the Obama administration was doing about jobs, about the economy, about health care, about the housing crisis, you didn't hear from those agency leaders who had expertise in what we were doing. Too often, we heard instead from White House political hacks reciting talking points about work that they really weren't doing and often did not understand. And frequently, the primary spokesperson was the president himself.

In his first cabinet meeting after he was reelected, President Obama apologized. Basically, he said—and this was his reflective moment of taking stock of want went wrong—"I appointed some amazing people to be my cabinet secretaries, but when it came to communicating about what we're doing well to address issues, I didn't utilize your expertise and leadership. I will do that in the second term."

That realization and commitment to his cabinet was the president's equivalent of an after-action report. President Obama showed recognition of another important presidential leadership lesson about growing through adversity: you have to raise leaders up along with you and allow them to lead.

> **President Obama showed recognition of another important presidential leadership lesson about growing through adversity: you have to raise leaders up along with you and allow them to lead.**

As a leader, you own the accountability, but you share the responsibility. If something doesn't go right, it's on your shoulders. You don't blame your team for things not going well, but you give them part of the responsibility to help accomplish the mission, allow the team to succeed, and figure out how to get better.

CHAPTER 10
CREATE A LEGACY
OF LEADERSHIP

At the age I am now, if I can't teach, I shouldn't
even open my mouth to speak.

—Public Enemy, "RLTK"

D r. Myles Munroe, a pastor from the Bahamas and a world-renowned faith leader, said, "Success without a successor is a failure."[25] If we don't use our gifts, our talents, our positions as leaders to leave something behind for those who come along after us, then we may have been success-ful, but we will never be significant. We will not have finalized impact leadership. The goal of a leadership legacy is defining what we want to be known for long after we have departed from the organizations that we lead.

---

25   Dr. Myles Munroe, "Dr. Myles Munroe - No success without a successor," video, November, 22, 2014, https://www.youtube.com/watch?v=Am0jWmYedkg.

Your legacy is viewed through how you are remembered. Were you significant in the context of the organization? Answering the question of what can be done today that will have an impact on tomorrow is the critical definition of legacy. You've got to get the most out of every leadership opportunity. Getting the most means giving the most.

Leaders must have what I call an abundance mind-set. They can't have a scarcity mind-set. Scarcity mentality from a leadership standpoint is believing that you're limited in your resources and opportunity to have an impact. Some people are given a role or a title and believe the only thing they can do is their job; they can't control any other factors around them. To think in such patterns is to have a limited belief system. Leaders must adopt a mind-set that the organization and its mission are bigger than the leader and bigger than their role. They must be committed to transforming the role or transforming the organization.

Just as leaders cannot afford a scarcity mind-set of limiting beliefs, they can't employ scarcity language. Scarcity language is the language of minimization. It's the kind of language used by people like Coach Lawing and others I have discussed in this book. Some leaders use language that breaks others down, and many fail to speak in the big vision, big picture language required for organizations to grow and improve.

Leadership from abundance rather than scarcity creates leaders who have lasting impact and form the largest legacy. Such leaders don't hoard their power. They don't protect their positions; they share the power of their position. They grow beyond themselves and they sustain long-term thinking about their role, about their people, and about the organization. Their lasting impact will live on long after they have moved on through others who will continue to do the work. Great leaders recognize that they have succeeded when they have helped build organizations that no longer need them. The organization and its people will have become adaptive enough and so mission driven that the work will continue in the leader's absence.

Legacy is the opposite of a scarcity mentality. It starts with committing yourself to a higher purpose, seeing something greater in yourself than your role, and then acting like an owner and not a manager. To explain the difference, I turn back to football for an analogy. The Baltimore Ravens

Legacy is the opposite of a scarcity mentality.

have won two Super Bowls. The most recent was in 2013 when the quarterback was Joe Flacco. Football fans will all remember Joe Flacco because of how he performed in that game. He was a clear leader. Most people don't remember the quarterback for the Ravens when they won their first Super Bowl in 2001. Average fans don't remember Trent Dilfer because he was a manager and not a leader. He wasn't the most important part of the Ravens' offense, so the identity of the team wasn't attached to the quarterback. He didn't own the position and he didn't own the success or failure of the team. He stopped at managing his role. He became forgettable.

To leave a legacy, you can't be a custodian of your leadership role; you have to own it. That means you need to fill the position and man it and mine it as if it were the only position that you'll ever get again. That's acting as an owner and not a manager.

Part of ownership is taking a long-term view. A scarcity mind-set is about short-term thinking. The greatest leaders recognize that leadership is not built in a day; it's built over a lifetime. They process the experiences they have had over their lifetime and assess what from those experiences allows them to contribute to their organizations in the moment and long into the future. Such vision requires that you are intentional about your leadership legacy. You're intentional about your resources. You're intentional about your time. Your legacy is what you give to others in terms of leadership capability, leadership opportunity, leadership effectiveness, leadership impact, and leadership responsibility. Committing to all these things characterizes the mind-set of a true owner, along with taking a long-term view, and being intentional with time and resources.

I have tried to be intentional with the people who have been important in my life. As an older brother—five years older than Cherone—I was always aware of how he looked up to me, which is a natural thing for younger brothers. I tried always to pour the best of myself into Cherone, whether that was sharing our mutual love of hip hop or giving him honest advice. At the *USS Cole* memorial service, a number of young guys who served with him came up and hugged me, saying that Cherone had spoken of me frequently and credited me with teaching him about music: "We just want to meet the man who blessed Cherone because Cherone blessed us." I've tried to do the same with my twin brothers Jamal and Jason.

And I've tried to do something parallel with a number of people who have served under me in the organizations I have run. I've intentionally tried to give people chances and empower them because I am so very aware of how I am a living legacy created by people such as Lenora Bush Reese. It's a way of paying it forward. I think of young people I have brought along, interns including Seante Hatcher, Somayah McKinny, and Stephen Graves. I think of people I have mentored, including Ramon Looby, Mayor Terrance Culbreath, and Sam Johnson, whom I met when he was nine years old and who just finished his final year of law school. As an undergraduate, Sam interned with me at the statehouse and later worked as my legislative aide. I then recommended him to my friend Steve Benjamin, when he was running for mayor of Columbia. Sam worked on Steve's campaign and then joined his administration as a special assistant.

My campaign body man was Heyward Harvin, who also went on to work for Mayor Steve Benjamin, and now, in Steve's second term as mayor, also serves as a special assistant.

I think of women such as Mia McLeod, whom I convinced to run for my legislative seat when I stepped aside to work at HHS. I gave Mia all of my donor lists, all of my e-mail network and volunteer lists, anything I could offer her to help her be successful. She won the seat and has served South Carolina and her constituency so incredibly well. She now serves in the South Carolina Senate.

When I think of Mia's intelligence and drive and devotion to service, I can't help but think of a woman such as Natalia Cales, who grew up in foster care because her mother had died from the HIV/AIDS virus. After graduating from college, Natalia started a nonprofit that focused on helping teens and adolescents develop healthy sexual behaviors and worked on AIDS education and prevention. I hired her at Fair Share as a community organizer for health care; she would work days for Fair Share and volunteer nights on the Obama campaign. Once I was at HHS, I had the opportunity to hire a regional outreach specialist focused on the ACA, so I brought in Natalia. She is now the executive officer for Region IV and has, in the past, been detailed to the CDC to run operations for an HIV/AIDS outreach program in Zambia. In her current capacity, among other duties, she is involved in hurricane recovery efforts in her native Puerto Rico.

Though younger when I met her, Natalia is not so different from someone such as Candace Hamana, whom I met when she was volunteering on the Obama campaign. She was the wife of an army veteran, a full-time college student, and the mom of a fourteen-year-old son. Seeing her skills, I brought her onto my campaign, where she organized my grassroots efforts. A Hopi, Candace has now moved back to her native Arizona and works as a senior policy official representing her tribe.

I cannot mention the names of everyone for whom I have tried to provide opportunity and leadership development. They are too numerous. I have listed the ones above as an illustration of my lifelong commitment to building a legacy. However, I cannot conclude this point without also mentioning one last person, my daughter Ashley. One day, without doubt, she will be my most important legacy. She's thirteen at the time of this writing. She's incredibly bright, athletic, an all-around phenomenal person. She doesn't yet understand the method to my madness when I try to teach her about leadership and values and the importance of serving others. Most of the time, I'm still just Dad to her. As I often say when I'm speaking on the topic of leadership, my toughest leadership challenge ever is raising a daughter, for through Ashley, I've gotten to prove my concepts about the value of service and the meaning of empowerment. Each day I must balance her need to be independent

Through Ashley, I've gotten to prove my concepts about the value of service and the meaning of empowerment. Each day I must balance her need to be independent and my desire that she recognizes she has an awesome responsibility to lead and have an impact on others.

and my desire that she recognizes she has an awesome responsibility to lead and have an impact on others.

For that is what I feel: an awesome responsibility for others. Just as I have had an impact on people in my life, I have tried to change and better the organizations I have served. You can do the same, for real leadership leaves a lasting mark on those organizations you lead, and it's true in the actions those organizations take and the outreach in which they participate. I played my small role in implementing the ACA and in helping people see the value and change it could bring to their lives. And no matter how much others rewrite the law or try to repeal portions of it, once people feel the reality of legacy in their lives, they become invested in that legacy. With the ACA that means there are aspects that will forever be part of a new American vision for health care, things such as the right to never be denied coverage because of a pre-existing condition; or, due to a mistake on an application, the right to prescription benefits or maternity care; or the realization by hospitals that health care is no longer about continuing to treat people the same way and expecting a different outcome. These are among the legacy features of the ACA and of Barack Obama's will to take action to improve the lives of America's citizens.

The legacy of Lenora is me. The legacy of me exists within the people I have invested in for the future—their future and *our* future together. Success without a successor is a failure.

PRESIDENTIAL PRINCIPLE NUMBER SEVEN
Work Today for Tomorrow's Impact

In the way that I am confident many of the vital elements of the ACA will stay with us and grow into ever-improved legislation in the future, the Family Medical Leave Act (FMLA) of 1993 initiated and fought for by Bill Clinton, has reached a place of permanency and expectation today. The FMLA is an integral part of life in America. As all laws are, it is imperfect. Just as imperfect but as meaningful as when Bill Clinton left a summit early to return home and comfort us and the other families of the *Cole* attack victims. And as with all laws, for as many people who have benefited from it, there are others, particularly employers, who remain frustrated with its demands. But no matter your vision of the law, it has changed lives, so much that many cannot imagine living without it.

When my mom lost her son on the USS Cole, the FMLA allowed her to take time away from work and not worry about losing her job while she grieved for her son and met the needs of her surviving family.

The FMLA requires covered employers to provide employees with job-protected and unpaid leave for qualified medical and family reasons, including pregnancy, adoption, foster care placement of a child, personal or family illness, or family military leave. If you are a full-time employee working for a company that employs fifty or more, you're entitled to twelve weeks of unpaid leave during a twelve-month year to deal with your medical needs.

It applies to you, your parents, your spouse, and your children. It means that when a crisis strikes, you keep your job. The law was passed based on common-sense belief. Its formation was mostly driven by women. There were large numbers of women joining the workforce, and Clinton wanted to support working families. When my mom lost her son on the *USS Cole*, the FMLA allowed her to take time away from work and not worry about losing her job while she grieved for her son and met the needs of her surviving family.

Because the FMLA can make it hard for an organization to function at full capacity, it has caused employers frustration and certainly can create very real demands if an organization has a large number of employees out on leave at the same time. Some employers have responded by misusing the regulations, misrepresenting their purposes, or openly violating the law. But despite the abuses of some employers, employees have come to value the law's presence. And most recognize that the goal of the law is to provide meaningful support to families and to improve long-term health outcomes. In many instances, its presence has changed lives.

Medical leave for families was an important part of Bill Clinton's campaign agenda, and so the FMLA was introduced on the first day of the congressional session in January 1993. Thirty days later, Bill Clinton signed it into law. Its passage speaks to a leader's commitment to doing something and putting everything on the line for it and getting it done. This aspect of his legacy has lasted twenty-five years. The FMLA shares a legacy with similar commitments that have stood the test of time, largely because of the underlying logic behind their formation and because of being widely embraced by the public. In this regard, it is legislation that bears a resemblance to Franklin D. Roosevelt's creation of Medicare or Social Security, mechanisms for ensuring health care and financial savings for the elderly that never

THE PRESIDENTIAL PRINCIPLES

before existed. The best legislation is the legislation that everybody can identify with. Whatever one's politics, the FMLA empowers people, as Medicare does, providing them with the capacity to care for themselves and their loved ones rather than being indiscriminately fired or abandoned to die in old age. On the maternity front alone, the frequency of leave went from 37 percent to 93 percent just in the years Clinton was in office.[26] Imagine the impact those maternity leaves had on the health of mothers and their babies, on the well-being of families, and on the early bonding and development of infants. Measure those benefits against a mother returning to work a few days after her delivery—days likely without pay if she were poor—and immediately placing that infant in a daycare. Bill Clinton labeled the benefits of laws such as the FMLA as "empowerment through opportunity and responsibility."[27]

Part of Bill Clinton's legacy exists in the actual lives of countless individuals, not just in the vision to form a policy and the dedication to see it passed into legislation. It exists in every son or daughter who knows that they can take time off work to go visit their ailing parents. It exists in every parent who needs to be at the hospital to spend their last days with their child who is terminally ill with cancer. It exists for the parent who has exhausted all of her sick leave attending appointments and surgeries for her child so that now she can celebrate with that child on a trip to Disney World with the Make a Wish Foundation. It exists in the couple who has spent years waiting to adopt a child and can spend their first weeks as a family together. These are the real measures of legacy.

---

26   Bill Clinton, "Why I Signed the Family and Medical Leave Act," Politico, accessed June 26, 2018, https://www.politico.com/story/2013/02/the-family-and-medical-leave-act-20-years-later-87157_Page2.html.

27   Ibid.

CONCLUSION
LASTING IMPACT

We closed the last chapter looking at moments of lives changed by the lasting legacy of the FMLA and its success because of Bill Clinton's leadership. You may look at this sort of legacy and think, *But I'll never be president. I can never have that kind of an impactful legacy.* But the truth is you can have presidential impact without being president. You can change the organizations you serve, and you can create legacy in others that will live on. It's not about who is leading but how they lead. By applying the presidential principles that have been the focus of this book, you can become an impact leader. It starts by transforming your vision of your role and seeing yourself as serving others. Once you see your role as a servant-leader, then you will recognize the value of empowering those around you. Do that well enough, with sufficient intentionality and a keen eye on the mission you are trying to complete together, and within those you empower you will leave a lasting legacy.

It's easy to look at some the problems we face in politics and across myriad industries and organizations and think that we are doomed, but I feel entirely the opposite. Great leadership is obtainable. And with great leadership, organizations can have great outcomes. Just as we can learn lessons about leadership from US presidents, each of us can have a presidential impact on our organizations if we commit ourselves to following these principles of leadership. I'm so much better because of my experiences with George Herbert Walker Bush, Bill Clinton, George W. Bush, Barack Obama, and Donald Trump (read the epilogue for my experience), even when I have disagreed with them on specific approaches or in certain circumstances. Just as we discussed when examining growth through adversity, we can learn from others' mistakes (and our own) as well as their successes. I've grown by examining the different approaches to leadership displayed by each of these men and by having their lives touch my own. I am better for reflecting on the encounters I have had with them. This book has outlined some of what I have learned. My desire is for you to benefit from these lessons as well. My goal has been to give you the tools to become the difference maker in the lives of those who make a difference around you.

You have a great leader inside you. If you ever doubt that you can have impact, look no further than those you serve and those you hope to serve in the future. Having read this book, you have a blueprint you can apply in your life. Take from it what you can and pass it along. Give the book to someone else. But most importantly, if its ideas resonate within you, pass them along. Become the impact leader who impacts the lives of those who impact others. Everyone deserves to have a leader who inspires action and creates a lasting impact, such as Lenora Bush Reese and Barack Obama. You are capable of being that leader.

EPILOGUE

Losing my brother at the hands of terrorists is one of the most painful things that could happen to a person. However, this same painful tragedy has provided me a powerful opportunity to bond with other American families who have similar experiences of grief and loss. We are called Gold Star Families. Having this Gold Star has offered me incredible opportunities to meet with some of the most important leaders in our nation. I have been able to distill some important leadership lessons from my experiences. In this book, I have outlined stories and experiences with four of the five US Presidencies. These presidencies have had the most impact on my leadership journey. As a final note, I want to share a brief lesson from my 2018 encounter with my fifth presidency, President Donald Trump and Vice President Mike Pence.

My family and I were invited to a reception in honor of Gold Star Families at the White House. It was an opportunity for the President and senior White House officials to honor and remember, those who gave their lives in military service. My mother, Jamal, Jason, and I were granted a private meeting with Vice President Pence and we were later introduced to President Trump. Both meetings were our chance to share with them our family's commitment to service embodied by Cherone's sacrifice for our nation. The meetings were a sharp contrast. The first meeting with the Vice President was thoughtful, intentional, and consistent with the third presidential principle. Mike Pence decided to engage. He listened to our family's story and he shared his story. The second meeting with President Trump couldn't have been more different. The whole encounter felt insincere and superficial. We stood eighteen inches away from the President of the United States but it might as well have been eighteen hundred miles away. He was physically there but his conversation was absent of thoughtfulness, meaning, and intention. I walked out of the room feeling that our story meant nothing to him. Our words had no impact on him as a human being, as a leader, and definitely not as a commander-in-chief. He showed no empathy about my brother's sacrifice. He didn't engage about our experiences as a Gold Star Family. His words and actions didn't empower us to a greater sense of service. It seems as if he didn't care about the service or the sacrifices that have been made by those in uniform. As I stated in the third presidential principle: the best leaders are the ones who listen, learn, and care for those they lead. This principle should be the prerequisite of any commander-in-chief.

REFERENCES

THE THIRTEEN BOOKS THAT ENCOURAGED ME TO TAKE ON THE RESPONSIBILITY OF LEADERSHIP

- *The Message to A Black Man in America* by Elijah Muhammad

- *The Autobiography of Malcolm X* by Alex Haley

- *Makes Me Wanna Holler* by Nathan McCall

- *The Spook Who Sat By the Door* by Sam Greenlee

- *How People Get Power* by Si Kahn

- *The 21 Irrefutable Laws of Leadership* by John C. Maxwell

- *Who Moved My Cheese* by Spencer Johnson

- *The Leadership Challenge* by Posner & Kouzes

- *Team of Rivals* by Joyce Kearns Goodwin

- *The Art of War* by Sun Tzu

- *Purpose Driven Life* by Rick Warren

- *The Audacity of Hope* by Barack Obama

- *The Audacity of Leadership* by Anton J. Gunn

THE 11 TOP WRITINGS THAT IMPACTED MY LEADERSHIP APTITUDE

- Martin Luther King, Jr., "A Letter from a Birmingham City Jail"

- Fredrick Douglass, "What to the Slave is the Fourth of July"

- David Brooks, "At the Edge of the Inside"

- Aristotle, Politics, Book I, Chapters 1-7

- The Declaration of Independence

- Dwight D. Eisenhower, "In Case of Failure Message"

- George Orwell, "Shooting an Elephant"

- Universal Declaration of Human Rights

- Ted C. Fishman, "Making a Killing: The Myth of Capital's Good Intentions,"

- The Book of James, *The Bible* (NIV)

- "In the Ghetto," Lyrics by Eric B & Rakim

THE 11 TOP WEB RESOURCES FOR A BETTER LEADERSHIP ATTITUDE

- Psychology Today Blog, *Clear, Organized, and Motivated* by Jim Stone (https://www.psychologytoday.com/blog/clear-organized-and-motivated)

- *Harvard Business Review* (https://hbr.org/topic/leadership)

- Forbes Leadership Blog (https://www.forbes.com/leadership)

- Robert Kiyosaki, (http://www.richdad.com/)

- Family Life (https://familylife.com)
- Les Brown, "Get Your Mind Right"
- Jim Rohn, "Your Best Year Ever-Personal Development Training"
- Chimamanda Adichie, "The Danger of A Single Story"
- Jason Walker, Leadership Cures on Twitter (www.jasonwalker.com)
- John Maxwell Team on Twitter (https://twitter.com/JohnMaxwellTeam)
- Inc. Magazine on Twitter (https://twitter.com/Inc)

TOP 11 MOVIES THAT TAUGHT ME LESSONS ON LEADERSHIP

- *Twelve Angry Men*, 1957
- *Heart Break Ridge*, 1986
- *Glory*, 1989
- *A Few Good Men*, 1992
- *Malcolm X*, 1992
- *Pulp Fiction*, 1994
- *Braveheart*, 1995
- *Crimson Tide*, 1995
- *13 Days*, 2000
- *Remember the Titans*, 2000
- *A Long Walk to Freedom*, 2013

OUR SERVICES

A nton J. Gunn and the 937 Strategy Group provides trusted training and development services for front line and executive team leaders in the healthcare and human services industry. Our goal is to help individuals and organizations capitalize on opportunities to add value, improve outcomes, and increase engagement for their clients and customers.

We strive to impact and transform the healthcare landscape by helping established and emerging leaders to succeed.

Our expertise includes:

- Executive Leadership Development

- Team Building & Employee Engagement

- Succession Planning

- Public Policy (Healthcare & Human Services)

- Alliance & Partnership Development

- Stakeholder & Consumer Engagement

- Strategic Communications

- Public & Government Affairs

- Diversity Management

THE PRESIDENTIAL PRINCIPLES

Connect with Anton

LINKEDIN   https://www.linkedin.com/in/antonjgunn/

TWITTER   @AntonJGunn

INSTAGRAM   @AntonJGunn

FACEBOOK   https://www.facebook.com/AntonJGunn/

WEBSITE   www.AntonGunn.com